THE TECHNIQUE OF SHORT SELLING

THE TECHNIQUE

OF SHORT SELLING

Making Money on Declines in the Stock Market

by Mark Weaver

REVISED EDITION

With Appendix by The Editors of *Indicator Digest*

AN INVESTORS' LIBRARY PUBLICATION

DEDICATION

To the Perpetual Bull who, through pride of opinion and stubbornness, takes the mental defense that he is an "investor" during a Bear Market.

To the emotions of men that such emotions may be subdued, disciplined and controlled, in order that sane analysis and logical reason may be applied to investment commitments.

To the New Generation of Investors and Suppliers of venture capital without which our economy cannot grow or thrive. May they act with wisdom.

To the Short Seller, that he may by his operations, contribute to more orderly and stabilized security markets through the demand for and supply of securities which he creates.

PUBLISHERS' PREFACE TO 1963 REVISED EDITION

Mark Weaver's treatise on short selling technique, one of the few comprehensive studies ever written on the subject, has been known mainly to a limited circle of market traders since its first appearance in 1949. The work was intended as the first of 12 monographs on various aspects of stock trading and investing; unfortunately, this was the only one to be completed by Weaver before his untimely death of a heart ailment early in middle life.

Mark Weaver was educated in economics, finance and banking at Ohio State and Columbia, and was a registered Investment Counsel in California. He estimated that up to 1948 he had spent at least 8000 hours at statistical, graphical and technical research on the market, and that throughout the last 25 years of his life he had kept up hundreds of individual stock charts and several averages.

Weaver lived through the market panics of 1929, 1937 and 1946, and his intensive study during those periods helped him formulate the timeless principles set forth in this book. Although the first edition appeared 14 years ago, it is remarkable that most of the material is still pertinent to today's conditions; during the large 1962 decline, for example, much of Weaver's work could have been used to profitable advantage. We suspect that the market wisdom expressed here will apply as long as stock exchanges and stock traders exist.

A bare minimum of deletions have been made from the original edition, and virtually nothing has been added except for four timely Appendices which treat with current technical aspects of the market.

PREFACE

This book has been written for a particular group of investors, speculators and serious minded students of financial investments who have a desire to add to their store of knowledge and experience in the art of profitable prediction.

The particular intent and scope of the contents is to open up new avenues of thought, methods of interpretation and analysis of the complete business and financial cycles, consisting of both the broad upward surges or bull markets and the shorter but more drastic surges of bear markets. The intent is to present sufficient proven techniques and market strategy to enable the perpetual bull or investor to properly evaluate his investment position at a time when proper analysis of the security markets spells "out" in unmistakable conditions; that the bloom is off the bull market and that a long period of deflation in business and security prices is imminent.

It contains an explanation of the strategy and techniques for short selling which makes possible the making of money in a declining stock market. A complete understanding of such techniques and strategy, when properly utilized, will open up a complete new field in which the investor or speculator may operate. Lacking such knowledge, the investor-speculator will generally remain a perpetual bull who rides high during bull markets, but who holds on to his securities, as an involuntary investor, during the devastating declines of bear markets. It is he who, in many instances, will sell out near the bottom with large losses when his mind is overwhelmed with fear.

The subject matter is condensed in such a manner as to

reduce the material to only the essential requirements of short selling, and such other related observations and material as may be pertinent to a working knowledge of the business cycle and stock market operations.

It is presented with the purpose of opening the minds of thousands of investors who are totally unaware that short selling opportunities exist, and unaware of the possibilities for capital appreciation which exist in declining security markets during deflationary periods of recessions or depressions.

Much of the essential substance of the contents has been gleaned by personal experience as an investor and trader over a period of seventeen years. Much, in addition, has come from research on the experience of other successful investors and traders who have made profits in market operations over long periods of their mature lives. This includes men, both living and dead, whose mature years have been concentrated upon the protection of capital, its management and utilization during the periodically reoccurring booms and depressions over the long years of American industrial growth.

Anyone attempting to set forth any criteria for an analysis of stock market movements or the business cycle must draw much from the historical past. He must glean it from his own experiences and the practices of successful investors, speculators and counselors, whose long experience has made correct analysis and timing possible. He must present the evidences of his research, experience and psychological approach with quite a degree of humility, knowing that what he presents must be primarily governed by the constant evaluation and analysis of the emotions and reactions of the mass human mind and how it will react, en masse, to a given set of economic circumstances.

The value, understanding and wisdom derived from this work will depend upon the amount of study and thought given the various subjects. For those whose understanding and experience is yet small, it is suggested that they apply the principles and observations made herein over a testing period, making only small commitments to determine how accurately they are applying the observations, rules and proper psychological approach as herein outlined.

It is my sincere desire that this study will open up a new avenue of thought for the better utilization and protection of the reader's capital, particularly during the depression periods which inevitably come to a vigorous America which suffers periodically from growing and overexpansion pains.

THE AUTHOR

CONTENTS

Publisher's Preface vii
Author's Preface ix
Short Sale Defined 1
The Scope of Short Selling 1
Two Parts to a Transaction 5
How a Short Sale Is Consummated (DIAGRAM) 6-7
Cash and Stock Dividends and Rights 8
The Costs of Short Selling 8
Bulls Pay Interest—Bears Do Not 10
Loaning Stocks for Premiums 10
Remaining Long in a Bear Market 11
Short Selling "Against the Box" 13
Shorting "Against the Box"—Tax Advantage 14
Dividends and Premiums on Short Sales Now Deductible 15
The Short Interest 15
The Technical Position 18
Shorting "At the Market" 24
Which Stocks to Sell Short 26
Shorting Small Capitalization Stocks 28
The Short Covering Rally 30
The Stop Order for the Bull 34
The Stop Order for the Bear 38
Conditions Ending a Bull Market 40
Conditions Ending a Bear Market 44
The Dow Averages 47
The Dow Theory 48
Tape Reading 52
The Buyers' Strike 61
The Business Cycle 63
Timing the Business Cycle 65
Don'ts for the Bull 67
Don'ts for the Bear 68
Conclusion 70
Appendix by The Editors of *Indicator Digest* 71
   A. Sell Signals at Bull Market Peaks 72
   B. How to Select the Best Short Sale Candidates 75
   C. Short Selling from Charts, Using Volume as a Guide 77
   D. "Creeping" Shorts 80
   E. The "Panic Level" in Short Selling 81

THE SHORT SALE DEFINED

A short sale is one in which borrowed securities are used for delivery to the buyer. The sale is not complete until the seller discharges his obligation to the lender by delivering to him securities to cover the short sale.

A short sale is a debt contracted in goods rather than in money. If the short sale is made in a security market, the debt contracted would be in securities. If the short sale is made in commodity markets, the debt contracted would be in commodities.

THE SCOPE OF SHORT SELLING

A few simple examples of short selling are cited below in order to demonstrate the extent to which short selling affects most business relationships. As each example is described, the reader will realize that he or she, personally, has been engaging in short selling, possibly without realizing it. It is almost impossible for a person living today, who engages in normal activities, to be free from involvement in a short sale.

A publisher who accepts subscriptions for a monthly magazine at a specific yearly subscription rate has sold short. He has sold a periodical which he has, as yet, not edited or printed. Having sold the subscriptions, he must buy paper, ink and printer's services from month to month in order that he may produce a magazine for monthly delivery. If the cost of materials and labor rises above the subscription price, he will lose money. If, however, the cost of these materials and labor declines during the year, he will make a profit equal to the amount of the decline, over and above his normal operating profit.

A lawyer accepts a retainer fee from a corporation. He has sold his services short. He covers his short sale when he delivers agreements which are drawn at the request of the corporation.

One of the first recorded evidences of a short sale was that of Esau in Biblical times who sold his inheritance, which he did not own, to his brother for a meal of pottage.

A consulting engineer accepts a retainer and signs a contract with a corporation for future consultation services. He has sold his services short.

A staff doctor or surgeon in signing a contract with a hospital or clinic has sold his services short.

A purchaser of an automobile on a deferred payment or installment contract has sold his future earning ability short.

A school teacher signs a teaching contract which guarantees her five thousand dollars for the term of nine months. She has, on the date that she signed the contract, sold her ability and services short. During an inflationary period, when the cost of living items rises rapidly, she loses, due to selling her services short, but during a drastic deflationary period when wages and salaries of others are being reduced, she is protected by her contract and, therefore, has profited by selling her services short.

The Post Office Department sells a five cent stamp. In

doing so it has sold short and will be required to make a deferred delivery at the time the stamp is affixed to a letter and it is mailed.

A landlord anticipates a general decline in the rental value of his unit, due, as he sees it, to a current building boom. In order to protect himself against this rental value decline, he prevails, if possible, upon his renters to sign long term leases at current high rental prices. When such a lease is signed, the landlord has sold short. He must furnish for the duration of the lease deferred services, maintenance and repair. If his calculations regarding declining rental values and maintenance costs are correct and such declines do occur, he will have profited by the lease or short sale.

General Motors accepts an order for ten diesel locomotives at a contracted price. It has sold short because the locomotives are non-existent and must be fabricated and assembled for later delivery.

A housewife purchases a refrigerator on the installment or deferred payment plan. In this case the housewife has sold money short. She has traded money, which she does not now have (otherwise she would have paid cash), for a refrigerator, expecting to get the money later in order to make the deferred installment payments. If, during the installment contract, the price of identical refrigerators advances (i.e., the purchasing power of money declines), she gains by the contract. If, however, the price of the refrigerator declines (i.e., the purchasing power of money goes up), she loses by having made the contract—or, as otherwise stated, by selling money short.

A person making any cash transaction has, in effect, sold purchasing power short. The person does not ordinarily know whether his dollars will be of greater or lesser value in the future. If the value of the dollar declines (i.e., the price of goods advances), he has profited by selling purchasing power short or by the cash transaction.

From the above examples it can be concluded that where money, credit, contracts and related activities of people are involved, it is difficult to conceive of a single mature individual who is not at this moment involved in some phase of short selling or the short sale. It is, therefore, logical to ask "Why this hesitation, this fear of selling short in the stock market?"

Many people are inhibited by lack of familiarity with the techniques of short selling. Many people fear that they will be wrong in judging the bear trend. Others have developed prejudices against short selling through lack of knowledge. People fear that which they do not understand. Still others feel that the risks are greater than they care to make. This no doubt is a carry-over from the stories of "cornered" markets of several decades ago when there was insufficient protection against such corners of the market.

With the advent of the Securities Exchange Act of 1934 many rules were applied to security trading which greatly reduced the hazard of short squeezes or partial corners. This is not to imply that the SEC rules make any guarantees against short squeezes, but they do have former pool operators now in their employ whose duty it is to ferret out any operations which may be in violation of SEC rules of trading.

The author does not wish to minimize the risk of losses which might occur from short sales which are not protected by "buy-stop" orders placed above the market. These orders are so placed that the short seller may calculate or know what his loss will be before he starts his short selling operation. That there has been more money lost in Wall Street through long purchases than through short sales cannot be denied. It is recognized that only those who cross the crowd make money in the stock market. Since the crowd or public

4

is predominately and almost perpetually on the bull side, it behooves the trader to know when to act with the successful minority. This successful minority contains, at the proper stage in the business cycle, a goodly portion of those who sell securities short.

TWO PARTS TO A TRANSACTION

Every transaction in the stock market, whether a long purchase or a short sale, consists of two parts. The first part of the transaction for the bull, who feels that an advance in stock prices is imminent, is to buy or get long of stock. The transaction is never wholly completed until the sale of this stock is made. The first part of the transaction for the bear, who feels that a sharp decline in stock prices is imminent, is to sell stock short. The short sale transaction is never wholly completed until the second part of the transaction, that of purchasing or covering the stock, is completed.

The simplest manner of describing the short sale in stock trading is to say that it is the opposite of buying first for later sale. The short seller must sell the stock first and he must buy it back at a later date. The question immediately arises, "How can I sell that which I do not own?" You may do this only because of your broker's facilities for borrowing stock certificates with which he is able to make delivery for you. When you have sold a stock short and your broker has borrowed a stock certificate and delivered it to the purchaser, the first part of the transaction is complete. There remains a second part of the transaction, that of providing your broker with an equivalent certificate at a later date, so that he may return it to the person or broker from whom he originally borrowed it.

In order to provide this certificate you must eventually buy an equivalent number of shares to cover your previous short sale. When this buy order is executed, the short sale

HOW A SHORT SALE IS CONSUMMATED

Note: This diagram is provided as background information, for the better understanding of the reader. In practice, one need not be overly concerned about the performance of the steps indicated, which are the function of the broker. With this explanation, however, the reader will more easily understand the statements of account rendered by his broker.

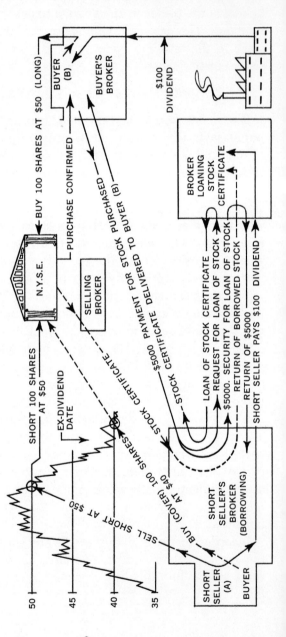

1. Short Seller A (extreme left) gives order to his broker to sell 100 shares at $50. This order meets buy order from Buyer B (extreme right). Confirmation of purchase goes to B's broker and to B. A's account is credited with $5000 when sale is confirmed.

2. B's broker pays A's broker $5000 for the stock. A's broker sends the $5000 to the lending broker (near right), who, with the $5000 as security, lends A's broker a stock certificate. This is delivered to B's broker and to B.

3. Short Seller later becomes a buyer (follow hatched line) and places order to buy ("covers" the short sale) at $40 per share. Order is executed and stock certificate is delivered to A's broker; the latter must now deliver the stock certificate to the original lending broker.

4. Upon receipt of the stock certificate, the lending broker returns the $5000 he had held as security to A's broker, and the short sale is completed.

5. Short Seller A's account is debited by $4000 for his covering purchase; his earlier credit of $5000 for the short sale, minus his $4000 debit, leaves him $1000 profit, less commission and tax. In addition, if the company whose stock is involved has declared a dividend during the time preceding A's delivery of the stock certificate to the lending broker, A must pay the lending broker the amount of the dividend ($100 as illustrated here); B receives his dividend from the company.

transaction is completed. If, for example, you sold a stock short at $50 per share and during a subsequent market decline, you bought or covered it at $40 per share, you would make a profit of $10 per share minus commission, interest and taxes. If the stock advanced above $50 and was covered above that price, naturally the operation would result in a loss.

CASH AND STOCK DIVIDENDS AND RIGHTS

The owner of the stock is entitled to all cash and stock dividends and rights. Since the short seller is short of stock, he is also, in effect, short of all cash and stock dividends and rights declared during the time he is short of the stock, and such dividends and rights will be debited against the short seller's account. This should cause the short seller no concern, as the market compensates the short seller by an automatic decline in the price of the stock in an amount equal to the dividend. This automatic decline is evident on each ex-dividend date.

THE COSTS OF SHORT SELLING

The known costs of short selling are the broker's commission, the sales tax and the short sales tax. Commission rates are the same as for buying stock and are based upon the money value of the transaction.

The Federal sales tax on stock sales was imposed during the first World War. Both the Federal and the New York sales taxes were levied to raise revenue, but a later Federal short sales tax was imposed to discourage short selling, particularly during periods of extreme deflation and declining stock prices. It was felt that such a tax would reduce bear raids on the market which were possible before the Securities Exchange Commission was established. Under present SEC rules these bear raids are impossible since a short sale can be made only on an advancing price (on an "up tick") from the last preceding price or at the same price which an advancing price established (on a "zero-plus tick").

A short sale can never be made at a price lower than the last preceding price (on a "down tick") nor at the same price established by a declining price (on a "zero-minus tick").

The unknown costs of short selling are dependent upon several factors: the length of time elapsing before the short sale is covered, the condition of the money market, and the availability of loanable stock.

A person may remain short of a stock as long as he desires, providing his brokerage account and arrangements are in good order. If you are selling short, your broker, who borrows a stock certificate for delivery as a result of your short sale, must deposit the current market value of the stock in cash to the account of the lender of the certificate. Under ordinary circumstances the lender of the certificate would be expected to pay the going rate of interest while he has the use of the money. However, when the demand is great for loanable securities in relation to the supply, the lender may refuse to pay any interest at all. In such a situation the stock is said to "loan flat." This is the usual case.

If the demand for the loan of stock on the part of the shorts becomes insistent, lenders of stock will demand a premium payment so that instead of paying interest to the borrower of the stock for the time the money is furnished, the lender of the stock will now not only have the use of the money furnished him without cost, but in addition will receive a premium paid by the borrower of the stock. The stock, under such circumstances, is said to be "loaning at a premium." When such premiums are demanded, they are debited to the short seller's account.

BULLS PAY INTEREST — BEARS DO NOT

On all long purchases of stock the broker must furnish funds for payment which are not provided by the margin. For these funds the bull must pay interest to his broker during the time he remains long of the stock. The bear, however, need pay no interest. His broker, having delivered the stock which was sold short, receives the funds from the sale which he immediately puts up with the lender of the stock. It can readily be seen that the broker does not furnish any of his own funds in handling the short sale and, therefore, charges his customer, the short seller, no interest.

LOANING STOCKS FOR PREMIUMS

On occasions, when premiums are being paid for the loan of stock, the holder of long stock may, through his broker, loan his securities for short sale delivery. If the premium is, for example, two dollars per day per hundred shares, one dollar per day will be kept by the broker for his services. The broker must secure the owner's permission before loaning any customer's stock for delivery as the result of a short sale.*

---

* Editor's note: This permission normally is granted as part of the agreement executed by the customer in establishing a margin account with his broker.

REMAINING LONG IN A BEAR MARKET
IS ILLOGICAL

There are many bulls who smugly assert that they are investors and not speculators or gamblers. That they do not gamble may be conceded, but that they do not speculate is highly improbable. Every investment is to some degree a speculation. A short sale can never be considered an investment; however, the capital appreciation resulting from successful short selling ventures may be as great or greater than the results of successful investment ventures on the long side of the market.

The investor is rare who is not a bull on his own particular investments. He, therefore, has capital appreciation as his goal as well as a return on his invested capital. In reality his purpose is much the same as the short seller whom he many times attempts to discredit. One great advantage, however, which the short seller has over the long purchaser of stock is that by being on the short side of the market he never can be forced by indecision to become an involuntary investor. This is not true of the bull investor.

An involuntary investor is one who has made a purchase of stock with two, and only two, ideas in mind. First, he thinks that the market and his particular stock will advance in price. Second, he wants to buy a stock which will pay dividends during the time required for his stock to advance. Having decided upon the particular stock he wishes to buy, he calls his broker and puts in a buy order. This decision is voluntary. It remains a voluntary decision as long as he has an opportunity of making a second decision to voluntarily sell at a profit. The stock advances and he is pleased with his selection. A time comes, however, when his commitment does not show him a profit, and he becomes a little disturbed at the poor action of the stock. The stock now shows him a small loss which seems to slightly disturb him. He should voluntarily sell and take his small loss at once. This he does not do. The stock moves lower and he is mentally restrained because of the amount of the loss he would be forced to take if he sold. Because of this large loss, his mind is not free to make a quick and correct decision as was possible when the loss was small. He has thus become an involuntary investor and will no doubt hold the "investment" hoping that it will not go lower in price. The "investment" at this time may show him a $500 loss, but the stock pays its $25 quarterly dividend regularly. Such a loss is equivalent to five full years of dividends, and yet he tells his friends that he made a "long pull" investment. His mind is not free from the emotions of fear and disgust during the required long pull, and subsequently he may sell out taking a very large loss. He was an involuntary investor because he had not learned to disregard the "investment idea" when his stock began to act poorly and when it showed him a small loss. Had he immediately decided to sell when the stock was acting badly, he could have done so with little emotion and his decision would have been voluntary.

The short seller cannot become an involuntary investor such as above described for he, at no time, owns any stock. He contracts a debt in the security which he sells short, and he is sometimes forced to cover when the price of his stock advances. In buying or covering his short sale he is completing the transaction and not beginning one as is the investor when he buys long stock. The short seller is always more alert regarding his position than the long buyer, and therefore, will take small losses rather than large ones. This attitude of not allowing losses of any kind to grow into big losses is a requirement of successful investment and speculation.

Remaining long of stock during a bear market for the

purpose of securing income is illogical. The purpose of investment is, first, to protect capital from depreciation in amount and value, and second to secure an adequate return commensurate with the risk involved. To protect capital from depreciation one must be willing to quickly admit errors when made, regardless of the dividends currently being paid on the stock or the income needed. One must be willing to sell stocks which show substantial profits, regardless of the need of income from them, when one discerns the exhaustion of a bull market and the possible change of trend.

It is quite logical for the investor to completely liquidate his holdings early in a bear trend, regardless of his need for income and to use, from his capital account, an amount equal to the income he previously secured from his invested capital. This plan will conserve his capital and result in its depletion only by the amount of its former yield, rather than the much greater depletion of his capital by rapidly declining prices had he remained long of stock.

SHORT SELLING "AGAINST THE BOX"

Short sales "against the box" are short sales which are made as a temporary convenience for future delivery. The short seller in this case is carrying long stock in his safety deposit box from which he can, in the future, make deliveries to cover his short sales. One reason for selling short against the box is that the investor may be on a trip or sea voyage, a thousand miles away from his bank and safe deposit box. He cannot immediately or physically make delivery of his long stock which he wishes to sell at current prices, so he sells an equal amount of the stock short, knowing that he will get the current market price for his stock, and that he can deliver his long stock from his deposit box to cover the short sales

13

when he returns from his trip. If the market has a drastic decline following the date of his short sales, he is, of course not affected by the decline, since during a portion of his trip he has been both long and short, and the loss on the long stock is offset by the gain on the short stock. He does not have a short position in this case, but has only sold short as a hedge against an anticipated market decline. In using a short sale against the box he is able to protect his long profits from sudden and drastic declines, which he may consider imminent as a result of a sudden break of unexpected bad news.

SHORTING AGAINST THE BOX
— TAX ADVANTAGE*

Shorting against the box is a valuable procedure in the reduction of capital gain taxes. A bull investor or trader who has made a long purchase, which has resulted in a considerable price enhancement in less than six months, can utilize a short sale in the same stock to much advantage. The price of his stock has risen to such a point that it shows a substantial profit, and he hesitates to sell it due to the fact that he has not held the stock for six months. To sell during a holding period of less than six months will result in a tax liability on 100 per cent of the capital gain, while to postpone selling until after the holding period of six months has elapsed will result in a tax liability on only 50 per cent of the capital gain. He consequently decides to sell an equal amount of the stock short in order to protect his profits until the holding period has elapsed. After the six months' period has expired, he covers his short sale by making delivery from stock which he held in his safe deposit box. If the price of the stock continues to rise after the short sale against the box is made, new

* Editor's note: Since 1950, tax regulations require that *all* short sale profits be taxed as ordinary income.

14

stock should be bought to cover the short sale and the old stock should be sold after holding more than six months. The loss on the short sale resulting from an advance in price can be used as a short term 100 per cent deduction against profits on the old stock, which due to completion of holding period now subjects those profits to only a 50 per cent tax liability.

DIVIDENDS AND PREMIUMS ON SHORT SALES NOW DEDUCTIBLE

A recent encouragement for the short seller has been provided in an income tax ruling issued by the government. The ordinary investor who sells securities short is now allowed to take a deduction for the amount of dividends which he must make good during the period he is short.

At first the government took the position that the payments of dividends by the short seller were not deductible as expenses of the short sale; however, in a series of court contests, the deduction for dividend payments was held allowable, first to regular dealers in securities, and then to those who buy and sell securities with sufficient frequency to be in the category of traders in securities. The government has now issued a tax ruling in which it grants the same deductions to the ordinary run of investors, regardless of frequency of trading.

The short seller must pay any premiums demanded for the loan of securities which he has sold short. These premiums, due to the recent tax rulings, now fall into the same category as the dividend payment while short, and also become a deductible item as an expense chargeable against the short sale.

THE SHORT INTEREST

The short interest is the term used to represent the total

number of shares, in all stocks, which have been sold short and which remain in short position as of a specific date.

The Dow-Jones News Service reports the total number of shares of the short interest usually on the third business day after the fifteenth of each month. The total number of shares which are short in specific stocks are given in comparison to their short interest of the previous month. Only stocks which have a short interest of 5000 shares or more are listed.

Knowledge of the amount of short interest in a stock is an aid in evaluating its technical strength or weakness. If, following a protracted decline, a stock has acquired a large short interest, it will have support from the short sellers who are always potential buyers on any further decline in the stock. This is particularly true as a stock declines and approaches a former important support level. If the stock fails to decline further and remains relatively firm, while at the same time the short interest greatly increases, you may correctly presume that further short selling, at this time or at this level, may be ill-advised and will undoubtedly be very costly.

After a rather long decline, in which traders and the public have been making profits on the short side, it is very dangerous to follow the short selling crowd. Beware! When short selling becomes too popular, a strong short covering rally may be near at hand. The reason for this is that as the stock declines, the frightened bulls dump their long stock and the bears sell short. When the stock has gone down to a level at which it will attract long buyers and long-pull investors, and has scared out all stock in weak hands (traders and speculators), there comes a time when the supply (selling) diminishes to such an extent as to be equal to the demand (buying), caused by long-pull investors and by shorts who may be beginning to cover their shorts. With this exact balance in demand and supply a turning point or reversal in trend is started. When the shorts see a lack of price change, accompanied by heavy volume, they sense the reversal and put in their buy orders, at the market, to cover their shorts. This causes the demand to greatly exceed the supply, and a swift short covering rally develops. The short seller who has placed a buy-stop order above the current price of the market will have his profits protected and his short sale covered automatically.

Knowledge of the totals of the short interest of all stocks combined is of value in determining the technical strength of the general market, for the same reasons as described above for the individual stock. When the short interest is large, the underlying strength of the market is evident and its technical condition is strong, although the market may appear to be weak. Studies have been made over the past 15 years of the relationship of the amount of the short interest to the average daily volume of sales, and the ratio resulting shows that when such a ratio exceeds 1.05 to 1, it usually has been followed by a strong recovery movement of some magnitude. During the 15 years studied, the ratio exceeded 1.05 to 1 nine times. Of the nine periods, seven such periods have resulted in a reversal in the downward trend and a general recovery movement.* This simply shows that when too many investors, traders and speculators are inveigled or lured into the position of following the crowd near the last phase of a decline or advance, they are proven wrong by characteristic market forces which are humanly generated at those levels.

It is for this reason that the successful investor or trader will follow a bull or a bear trend only to the point where bullish enthusiasm begins to get excessive, or only to a point where bearishness and pessimism begins to get excessive. It

---

* Editor's note: More recently, "short covering rallies" appeared after the Short Sale Ratio exceeded 1.40 or 1.50 to 1.

is essential to so direct your thinking and to so control your emotions that you will follow the trend, but become less and less bullish as stocks continue to advance, and that you will become less and less bearish as stocks continue to decline. The general public or unseasoned investor-speculators are not able to so control their thinking and for this reason they buy near the top and sell, through fright, near the bottom of the market movements.

TECHNICAL POSITION

The investor who bases his decisions to buy or sell solely upon an analysis of basic fundamentals—earnings, management, cash position, general financial conditions, etc.—is very much at a disadvantage in arriving at a decision to buy or to sell. At a time when he should be selling stock, the fundamental factors are strong, the earnings and dividends high and optimism overwhelming. These seemingly favorable factors make it difficult and almost impossible for him to make the decision to sell stock. At another time, when the fundamental factors are weak, when earnings are nil, dividends reduced or passed and cash positions impaired, there is nothing among the fundamental factors which will restore confidence or nurture an optimism sufficient to produce a decision to buy stock.

It is, therefore, necessary for the investor who wishes to take advantage of cyclical movements to reduce the weight which he has previously given to fundamental factors, and to give additional weight and analysis to the technical factors which are evident in many ways at the beginning and ending of bull and bear markets. These technical factors must be given an increasing amount of weight in the analysis after the bull or the bear market has been in force for some time, since a technical reaction in a bull market may be the beginning of a bear market, and a technical recovery in a bear market may mark the beginning of a bull market. Bull markets and bear markets alike are controlled by basic economic fundamentals, but the intermediate wave movements within those basic trends are governed and given their impetus by technical factors.

The following factors or conditions make up what is known as the technical position of the market or the technical position of an individual stock:

1. Floating supply
2. Overbought or oversold condition
3. Short interest
4. Brokers' loans—Margins
5. Sell-stop (stop-loss) or buy-stop orders
6. Absorption of new issues—Effect on money supply
7. Public psychology
8. Stocks in strong hands/Stocks in weak hands
9. Volume of sales
10. Action of the market or stock

(1) The floating supply is that portion of stock which is in brokers' hands. It consists of stock which has not been ordered out in the owner's name, and also consists of stock which has been bought on margin. The term "floating supply" is applied to convey the meaning that this stock is generally changing hands and is quick to come out upon the market with each small price advance or decline. Floating supply stock is trader stock or the stock of those who daily sit in the board rooms and buy or sell on small stock movements.

When the floating supply of stock is large, the technical position is generally considered to be weak, and a great demand for stock will be required to force the price up through constant and continual offerings. It is for this reason that the supply and demand factors at such a level will cause a line or other type of top formation to be made. After weeks or months of fluctuation, usually narrowing in the amount of the fluctuation as the time passes, traders being whipsawed by the stock's action will gradually lose interest and withdraw. With the withdrawal of each trader, the floating supply is reduced. Not until the floating supply is sufficiently reduced can a definite and extensive move be made out of the line or triangle coil which has been formed.

(2) An overbought condition may be most simply explained by using an example of one investor. This investor has $100,-000 available at a particular time to invest in stocks. When he thinks the time is right, he begins to buy and when he has invested all of the $100,000 he no longer has any buying power. If he is a margin trader, he may soon have bought his limit, and is no longer a force in creating a demand for stock, as he has no further funds to expend in that manner. Regardless of how bullish he may be, he cannot contribute to the demand factor, but due to his "overbought" position he can easily contribute to the supply factor by selling when he becomes frightened. He also contributes to the supply potential by placing sell-stops under his stocks. Multiply this investor's position by four or five million similar investors' positions, and it is evident that none of them can give the market any further demand impetus, but that all are in a position to give substantial supply impetus as the market begins sagging or declining tendencies.

An oversold condition arises when there has been a prolonged period of liquidation usually caused by declining trends, bad trade and business news and general pessimism. When the great majority of those investors and traders have liquidated or sold their stock and they no longer have any stock to sell, they can no longer contribute to the overwhelming supply factor which caused stocks to go down. They are now in a cash position and, therefore, the only manner in which they can contribute force to the market, if they are not short sellers, is on the bullish or demand side. It is abundantly evident that when a market is completely oversold, it can go in only one direction and that direction is up. When a stock becomes oversold prior to and at the time of bad news, such as an omission of dividend, the stock may have a rally when the bad news is out.

(3) The short interest described and discussed elsewhere in this material is an important technical factor for retarding further decline in price and for the stimulation of bullish moves. Each short seller is a potential buyer since he must sometime cover his short sale to complete his transaction. The shorts thus are the latent buyers who will create demand, when, from a study of fundamentals alone, there seems no logical reason for a recovery or advance in price. The market does not ordinarily nosedive when the short interest is large. To the contrary, such a large short interest has a stabilizing effect to check the decline and to start a reversal of trend.

(4) Brokers' loans, representing that part of the loans which are used to carry customers' stock on margin, are a very important technical factor. These loans primarily determine the size of the floating supply in the market and in individual stocks. Bull traders, who operate on thin margins, are quick—or should be quick—to dump their stocks when the market moves against them. Bear traders on thin margin will cover quickly when a market movement proves them wrong. When margin traders are numerous they will usually act very much in unison when important support or resistance levels are broken. This causes at one time an overwhelming supply or offerings of stock and at another time an overwhelming demand for stock.

(5) Sell-stop (stop-loss) orders and buy-stop orders, placed under the market and above the market respectively, are

important technical factors which influence market movements. Elsewhere in this material their use has been explained as a method for limiting losses and for "getting on board" when important moves begin. Naturally these types of orders are as important technically as the number of traders who use them or the volume of orders so placed. Many times the reason given for sharp breaks in the market is that the market was honeycombed with sell-stop (stop-loss) orders. At other times when swift rallies occur the reason given may be that the shorts were driven to cover. That the majority of shorts use close buy-stops is not mentioned, but the large number of these buy-stop orders is a technical factor of considerable significance.

(6) Absorption of new issues of stock by the public or by the underwriters reduces the amount of money available to bid up the prices of securities at or near the end of a bull market. The manner in which new issues of stock are absorbed or over-subscribed is one of the most reliable indicators as to the fundamental and technical condition of a bull market. If, after an abnormal out-pouring of new stock issues which the public has readily absorbed, a condition arises in which further issues offered for sale become "sticky," —in other words, they are no longer over-subscribed, no longer completely subscribed and must be re-offered several times—it is an indication that the public's appetite and the public's purse can no longer digest additional offerings of stock. This is almost a sure sign that the public no longer has sufficient funds to maintain the price of securities at their present high level, and that a crash of security prices is imminent. It behooves both the bull and potential bear to watch how each new issue, which is offered after a bull market has been in progress for some time, is absorbed by the public. If all other sell signals fail to convince the bull that he should retire to the side lines, this condition of new stock offerings

becoming "sticky" should really frighten him into quick selling action.

(7) Public psychology, both at the top of a bull market and at the bottom of a bear market, is an indication that many of the technical factors have reached a degree at which they will begin affecting the market's action. Public psychology is both a cause and an evidence of greatly weakened technical factors which will sooner or later change the direction of the trend, when accompanied by proper fundamental factors. If not accompanied by such fundamental factors, the reversal caused by the technical factors will be an intermediate and not a primary movement.

(8) Stocks are in strong hands when they are in the lock boxes of those who have bought for the long pull and for income. When stocks have traded for a long time at low levels the gradual absorption of the floating supply by investors has a tendency to prepare the market for an advance. This factor contributes to a strong technical position for stocks and for the market generally. Stocks are in weak hands when, as has been previously described, they are held on margin and in the broker's name. Such stock, being traders' stock, will soon be offered for sale, thus causing a supply of stock which becomes an important technical factor.

(9) Volume of sales is a factor in the technical position of a stock or of the market. High volume, accompanied by a late tape after a protracted rise in prices, does not indicate investment buying is taking place, but that emotional buying is being done, usually by those who can ill-afford to carry the stock. Under such circumstances it is evident that the stock is passing from strong to weak hands. On the other hand, a market which has been in a bear trend for some time may either take a last devastating plunge on heavy volume, or it may become a listless, sagging market with volume of sales dwindling so small that brokers cannot make their ex-

penses. Stocks pass from weak to strong hands in both types of market action. When the stock gets into the hands of those who have no intention of selling it, except in the remote future, the technical position is considered to have been strengthened.

(10) The action of the market or of a stock brings into play many of the factors described above. The response of a stock or the market to good or bad news will change peoples' attitudes toward the stock or the market generally. These changes of attitudes may have their immediate effect of changing the weight previously given to certain technical factors. The stock action and the market's action helps greatly in the diagnosis of the technical factors and their relative effects on the future market movements. If the stock or the market advances on increasing volume and declines on decreasing volume after a protracted decline, the action shows that the technical strength is such that a change of trend is generally taking place. To disregard the stocks and the market's action, and the technical conditions which make that action possible, is to disregard the most important aids in the intuitive art and the scientific approach to predicting stock price movements.

SHORTING "AT THE MARKET"

Short selling, as previously stated, must be done only after watchful waiting, during which time the candidates for short sales are chosen and their market action studied. These stocks should show less strength than the general market and they must, by breaking supporting levels during the distributing stage, establish the beginning of a downward trend. When this pattern is first discernable in quite a few stocks, there remains little time in which to get a short position in the market. It is, therefore, advisable, when your short sale candidates rally back up into their former support levels, that you place your short selling orders "at the market." You have analyzed the market; you have chosen the stocks which you wish to sell short; you have waited patiently for certain things to happen, certain indicators which make you assured that the bear campaign is the correct one. Why then use a limit order and chisel for ⅛ or ¼ point at this time, and risk the chance of not getting short on what you have reasoned will be a sizable decline?

An at-the-market order, at certain times, can be extremely painful to the short seller. This is a condition when, through hesitation and indecision, he delays his short sale until the crash begins. Since a short sale must be made on the uptick of the market, an at-the-market short sale may not be executed except during a weak eighth or quarter point rally four or five points below the price at which you anticipated getting off your short sale. Even this will be welcome when the crash is one of 25 to 50 points, but it is extremely disconcerting, to say the least, for the short seller when his order is executed during a late tape five points lower than recent quotations, only to find a temporary rally set in that may immediately show a loss.

If you cannot act in time, it is advisable not to act at all. However, it is the big surprise crash that is extremely profitable to the short seller, so it behooves him to get his short position established during the early weakness of prices that precede the drastic selling which causes the drastic declines.

An at-the-market order should be used for most short covering. A smart short seller is not risking the short side of the market for ¼, ½ or 1 point profits, so why should he use a limit order? When it is time to cover, it is time to cover without indecision or chiseling, otherwise paper profits from short sales vanish quickly.

The use of buy-stop orders above the market as protection

for short sale profits and to limit losses is in no way contradictory to what has been said about the use of at-the-market orders, for the buy-stop order is in reality a clever device for forcing the short seller to buy at the market when a certain price is reached.

WHICH STOCKS TO SELL SHORT

Careful consideration must be given to the choice of stocks as candidates for short selling. Generally, the best rule is to choose well-known and actively traded stocks. The fact that such stocks may pay dividends, which will be debited against the short seller's account, should not deter the seller from their choice. One must remember that the price of the stock automatically declines in like amount to the dividend, when the stock goes ex-dividend, so that the payment of the dividend is generally cancelled out in equal amount by the ex-dividend adjustment decline.

The principal reasons for selling well-known and actively traded stocks are that such stocks, once a downtrend has been established, will generate among the many holders and traders in the stock a feeling of despair and pessimism which tends to amplify itself and thus give impetus to the downtrend. This is primarily to the advantage of the bear who will want to cover his short sale during pessimistic, emotional liquidation, knowing that when he places his covering buy order, he can do so readily and very close to the current market price.

Relative strength and weakness of stocks in relation to their own group and to the market averages should be a prime consideration in the choice of a candidate for a short sale. A stock which is acting poorly in relation to its particular industrial or rail group, and which is acting marketwise much weaker by refusing to make new highs when its group and the market averages make new highs, should be listed for close scrutiny as to its subsequent action on setbacks. If such stock breaks former support levels, while its group and the averages receive support at a former support level, this weak stock should be the short sale candidate when the decision on the timing to sell short can be made.

Short selling commitments must be made with speed and alacrity from a predetermined campaign consisting of predetermined stock selections. The timing of the short sale is extremely important, and must be determined by the analysis of the phases of the business cycle and the action of the stock and the market. There must be evidence of overspeculation; of the market being overbought; of the market being technically weak, and above all, there must be the final evidence of a reversal of the bull trend in the stock and in the averages. This final evidence is apparent with the breaking of well-considered support levels, which determines the beginning of the downward wave of the price movement trend.

Stocks which refuse to rise in a bull market should be studied as short sale possibilities. That such stocks will not rise with other stocks is an indication that they do not have appeal to either the insiders or the public. When such is the case, there is generally something fundamentally wrong with the company's future fortunes as related to economic factors.

It must be remembered that stocks go up or down because they are put up or down by demand and supply. The demand or supply factors are based primarily upon the consensus as to the future earnings of a particular company. If a stock fails to make new highs when others in its group and the general market are making new highs, it is logical to interpret this as a weakness in that particular stock. Its appeal to the wise and unwise alike has diminished and, therefore, its particular sponsorship is lacking in force. This may mean that the insiders are "out" of the stock and will become interested in it again only at lower levels.

Stocks which have had extremely rapid run-ups following a long general bull market should be earmarked for short sale consideration. Such run-ups, made on extremely high volume, are usually the advertising stages for distribution of the stocks.

The short seller will find many short sale candidates other than recognized growth stocks which he may sell short. The statement that all stocks decline in a bear market is generally true; however, it is wise to avoid those which, because of their economic position, will tend to resist the down movement.

The short seller will do well to analyze the weak recovery movements in specific stocks as evidence of their lack of strength and their inherent weakness marketwise. A stock is extremely weak when it will not go along with a sharp secondary recovery movement in a bear market. Such secondary movements, after their initial impetus, usually become dull and inactive, and it is from such characteristic action that the bear should follow the Wall Street axioms, "Never sell a dull market short during a bull market," but "Always sell a dull market short during a bear market."

DIFFICULT AND DANGEROUS ASPECTS
OF SHORTING SMALL CAPITALIZATION STOCKS

It is extremely difficult to sell short in small capitalization stocks. Such issues usually have from 200,000 to 600,000 shares outstanding. The number of daily transactions in these stocks is very small; there even may be a day or several days between transactions. This, together with the fact that there is usually a large spread between the bid and ask price, makes it difficult for the short seller to get short of the market exactly at the time he wishes. If he puts his order to sell such a stock at the market, he must wait until the bid and ask spread close and a sale price is established. This sale may be his, it must be remembered, only if it is made on an advancing price, or at the same price which the advancing price established.

It is true that small capitalization stocks decline faster than larger capitalization issues, but this means little if one is unable to get a short sale off at a time when such sale should be made. Not only is it difficult to sell short in small capitalization stocks, but it is also equally difficult to cover the short position at the bottom of a move. The same wide spread between bid and ask prices is evident at the bottom, as well as, usually, the dearth of transactions which makes covering difficult. The short seller in such issues does not have the opportunity to judge turning points on volume considerations in his own stock, but must look to the more actively traded stocks to gauge the balance of supply and demand which may signal a reversal in the trend of the stock and the market.

It is far wiser for the short seller to choose actively traded issues for his short sales. These stocks have large capitalizations, and it is relatively easy to get the short sale off. When pessimism develops from price decline, it is likely to be accentuated due to the larger number of shareholders. The covering operation is very easy and without a great spread in bid and ask price, because an active market prevails in these larger issues.

It is inadvisable to sell short a "cat" or "dog" stock which has shown a persistent and prolonged strength. Usually too many traders consider it a "dog" and consequently a very large short interest may develop, which will be used by the bulls to provide the main bullish impetus (short covering) for the total move.

It is much more advisable for the short seller to sell active, well-recognized and generally popular investment and speculative stocks, which he thinks are of such caliber as to warrant being included in the Dow-Jones Averages, but which are not so included. These stocks will generally have wider price movements than those included in the Averages, due to the fact that they do not have the same "investment stock" reputation, nor are they priced by a premium demand, based upon their excellent long term earnings and dividend records. If the short seller is certain that the trend is down, he will have little difficulty in the choice of his stocks for selling short.

THE SHORT COVERING RALLY

In contrast to a bull market, the moves in a bear market will be much swifter and more drastic in their immediate effect on public confidence. The first drastic decline of a bear market smothers the optimism of the bulls who are usually caught completely unaware by the decline. The collapse of prices usually comes with such speed and goes to such depth that the market will become temporarily oversold. There remains, however, a great mass of bulls who think that any prices are bargain prices, if they are substantially lower than those previously attained. These bulls now think that stocks are cheap, and rush in with buy orders. These orders, together with short covering orders, cause an enormous demand which temporarily overwhelms the supply of stock for sale, and a sharp, rapid technical and short covering rally takes place. The more rapid the rise of this move, the more certain one can be that sizable short covering is being accomplished. Since public confidence has been completely shaken by the previous drastic decline, secondary liquidation soon makes its appearance as the price of stocks advance in a technical and short covering rally to a level where those whose confidence has been shattered can sell out at or near their purchase prices.

These sharp recovery movements rarely develop into sustained and prolonged advancing movements, primarily because a short covering rally does not hold. For this reason the exhaustion point of a short covering rally may be used by other short sellers to go short of the market.

After the first crashing decline in a bear market the averages and individual stocks will ordinarily fluctuate wildly and usually be accompanied by high volume of sales. Very frequently the tape will be late at the point where an overwhelming demand develops sufficient force to turn the market strongly upward. The following three or four days of rapid advance may find the averages up 12 to 15 points, with the tape again being late on the top day of this advance. New short sales and secondary liquidation at this level may quickly turn the market down for a 12 to 15 point decline, where a test of the previous low will be made. Wide oscillating price movements may continue at this level for some time while the financial community and the public are getting over their sudden case of stock market jitters.

Trading both on the long and short side during such wildly oscillating movements, following the initial crash, requires considerable tape reading experience and plenty of nerve and financial resources. It is impossible to know at what point during the decline sufficient buying orders will come into the market to overcome the tremendous liquidation that is taking place. Only by sitting on the tape constantly during such a period can one see the emotional battle between supply and demand taking place. Trading in such a market should be attempted only by those of long stock market experience.

Another type of short covering rally is one that appears during a slow steady downtrend. The downtrend in this case

31

is characterized by no violent declines, but by slow and persistent liquidation. Suddenly, for no apparent reason, a stock may have a swift short covering advance. The advance may open with a gap on the upside and reach proportions of extraordinarily heavy volume in the several days required for the surprise move. Since this move is an abnormal and surprising one, it must be viewed with suspicion. When such a violent short covering move appears to have spent its upward force, selling, both from long accounts by bulls and for a short position by bears, will usually prove to be the proper and wise decision. Applying logic to the interpretation of such an abnormal or sudden move, one needs only to ask himself the nature of the buying and selling.

Such violent advances are known to be caused by nervous and emotional short covering. The long buying accompanying the move will be done primarily by short term traders, and such stock will come back into the market within a few days. It, therefore, can be reasoned that an advance which gets the impetus for its strength from such sources cannot hold its gain, and such gain will ordinarily be completely lost within a relatively short time. The top of such a move is, therefore, a short selling level.

Short sellers can judge the levels at which secondary liquidation will come into the market by studying the previous chart action of stocks. When, through a combination of an oversold condition and short covering, a strong rally develops which carries the price of stocks up into the lower levels of a previously formed line or to previous support levels, the short seller can be reasonably sure that the stocks will have difficulty in advancing further due to the secondary liquidation which they will encounter. At such levels ventures on the short side are frequently warranted due to the mass emotional thinking of investors. How often have you heard the statement, "When my stock goes back up to where I can get out even, they can have it." Multiply this attitude by several million investors and one can realize how potent a force the secondary liquidation becomes as a deterrent to further price rises through former levels. This thought may give those who are bearishly inclined sufficient courage to try ventures on the short side.

The potential short seller must know the levels at which the bulls are likely to sell their stock, and he must know the levels at which the bulls are likely to buy stocks. He must also know the levels at which other short sellers will be inclined to sell stock short and at which levels they will be inclined to cover their short sales. To properly judge these levels it is necessary to study the charts on individual stocks. From these charts it is possible to arrive at conclusions as to the stock's possible behavior when it reaches a particular level. This possible behavior will be based upon the stock's previous action and the amount of stock that changed hands at that level.

From the individual stock charts, the short seller can determine what price and level will represent an approximate 50 per cent recovery point which a short covering or secondary movement should reach. If the 50 per cent recovery point is at the same level where stocks were previously supported and heavily distributed, the supply encountered there will stop the recovery movement and turn it down. In addition, the 50 per cent recovery movement will have exhausted a great deal of the technical strength of the advance. The 50 per cent recovery level will, furthermore, be attractive to those traders who wish to sell short.

It is obvious then that the approximate 50 per cent retracement point, which is caused by the law of action and reaction and various technical factors, becomes a point or level at which (1) secondary liquidation will come into the market, (2) the technical strength will have been impaired, and (3) the bears will consider the level proper for additional short selling.

These three factors are of such importance that they rate first consideration and analysis by the potential short seller. At this half-way recovery level the hazard of being wrong is reduced to such an extent by technical conditions, that he should have no qualms about short selling ventures so long as the market remains in a bear trend.

THE STOP ORDER FOR THE BULL

A stop order is an order which does not go into effect until the actual market price of the stock in question reaches a previously given figure. Immediately upon touching this figure the stop order goes into effect as a market order. As an example, you may puchase a stock at $25 per share after the stock has been selling in the 25-27½ range for some months. This stock, during all recent market weaknesses, has received support at the 25 level and has not broken below that figure. After having made these observations, you make your purchase at 25, expecting the stock to rally to at least 27½ and possibly much higher.

In order to follow the wise policy of "limiting losses," you immediately place a sell-stop order at 24, feeling that if the stock does not advance as anticipated, you would not want to take more than a one point loss in the stock. This one point loss is, in your mind, a premium that you are willing to pay as insurance against a much greater loss, should a sharp decline in the stock occur. Let us assume that the support level at 25 is broken on the downside, and that such a sharp decline occurs soon after you purchase the stock. When the price of the stock reaches 24, your stop-loss order becomes immediately effective as a market order. You may get a higher price for your stock if the stock rallies after the 24 price is reached, or you may get slightly less for your sale if the stock immediately sells lower than 24. At any rate you should be happy, at the cost of a small insurance premium, to be out of the stock since it has moved contrary to your prediction. If a sharp decline occurs, which is likely, since the important support level of 25 was broken on the downside, and such a decline amounts to as much as eight points, you will be particularly happy that your stop-loss sell order has made possible a small loss of about a point rather than an eight point loss.

In the commercial world among the successful merchandisers who carry large inventories, there is a very wise axiom, "The first loss is the best loss." The first loss in this case means that there is a realization that a small loss exists and that something should be done about it. To sell now would result in a small loss; to postpone selling in favor of later consideration and decision will usually result in a much greater loss. This axiom is identical to the first part of the Wall Street axiom, "Cut your losses short, but let your profits run," an axiom which must be followed for successful investment and trading.

Let us assume that your buy commitment at 25 was a more fortunate one and that the support level of 25 was not broken, but that the stock rallied through 27½, an important resistance point and resistance top of a line formation that had been many months in the making. The breakout of the line on the upside would be a verification of your previous assumption that the line was one of accumulation. Now, with the stock selling at 28, you should cancel the sell-stop order at 24 and move it up to 26. This will guarantee that, should the stock decline, you will suffer no loss of capital or commission costs. The stock, however, continues to advance to 31, where it runs into upside resistance from which it reacts to 28½, where support and rallying tendencies are in evidence. From 28½ it advances to 32, breaking the previous 31 resistance, and thereby beginning a wave-like uptrend that should continue for sometime.

At this point you should cancel your sell-stop at 26, and move it up so that it will be approximately one point under the last support point at 28½. Your sell-stop order would now be under the market at 27½. With each subsequent wave into higher ground and each subsequent reaction, you should move your sell-stop orders up and place them just under the last reaction support level. This method of protection is known as using progressive stop orders. It will protect profits as they accrue, and provide constant protection against losses from sudden and unforeseen reversals in the market.

Let us now assume that you apply an even better strategy than you did in the former example. A line or narrow fluctuation in the price of a stock means that either accumulation or distribution is taking place. While the stock is in this line, it is a wild guess as to whether the forces of accumulation (demand) or the forces of distribution (supply) will prove the stronger. Not until the stock moves decisively out of the line on the upside are you certain that the line has been one of accumulation, and not until the stock moves decisively out of the line on the downside are you sure that the line is one of distribution.

The astute bull will not buy when a stock is in a line since he does not know whether accumulation or distribution is taking place. If the breakout is going to be on the upside, he will wish to get long of the stock on the first strong breakthrough on the up side; so he places a buy-stop order just above the top resistance points, which form the line, believing that if the buying or demand forces are strong enough to break the four or five previous resistance levels making up the top of the line, that those forces will be sufficient to carry some distance in the direction of the breakthrough.

Having placed his buy-stop order ¾ to 1½ points above the line, he automatically becomes long when the breakthrough occurs. Naturally, he pays more for the stock than he would have, if he had bought the stock while it was in the line, but the extra cost is justified in the added peace of mind and greater assurance that his operation is a correct one. Subsequently, as the price of the stock advances in its characteristic manner of advance and reaction, he will protect his profits with progressive stops, which have been previously described.

In order that you may strictly adhere to the proven strategy of profitable stock market operations—that is, cut your losses short, but let your profits run—you must, as your stocks advance in price, restrain yourself from selling or being tempted to sell for small profits. You must not sell too soon after a move gets started, and you must allow sufficient time to elapse to assure a movement resulting in a sizable profit. Such profits should be protected by sell-stops placed under the market. Care must be taken, however, in placing the sell-stop orders so that you will not be "stopped out," resulting in a small profit.

There are many stock market traders who average being right no better than 50 per cent of the time, and still they make sizable profits from their operations. They first adhere to the rule of not making a commitment until they see the probability of a sizable move in the stock. Second, they refuse to take small profits when the movement is going in their favor. They hold for sufficient time, to allow large gains to accrue. Third, they are quick to take losses, thereby making such losses as small as possible. A loss in a stock is a sign of error. The stock trader can afford to admit errors and take small losses, which he knows will be much more than offset by the large gains which he must and will allow to accrue.

THE STOP ORDER FOR THE BEAR

The short seller should use stop orders for five distinct purposes.

1. He should use the sell-stop order, placed just below a line or below important support points, in order to get short of the stock immediately upon the breaking of the line on the downside.

2. He should use the sell-stop order to get short of a stock which has broken its major uptrend line on the downside.

3. He should use a buy-stop order, placed above his selling price of each and all short sales, in order to limit his loss to a predetermined amount, this amount representing an insurance premium which he is willing to pay to guarantee against a large loss.

4. He should use progressive buy-stop orders, placed above each recovery point in a downtrend, in order to protect his short profits.

5. He should, after a long downtrend, and after what he presumes to be a line of accumulation or bottom formation, use or place buy-double-stop orders above the market in order that his short position may automatically be covered and, at the same time, that he may secure, automatically, a long position when the recovery movement begins.

Stop orders can not be intelligently placed without the use of charts of the individual stocks in which the trader wishes to operate. The trader must know when, and in what stocks, a line is being formed. He must know how long the stock has been in the line. To intelligently place buy- or sell-stop orders, he must know the resistance level and support level which makes up the formation of the line. His buy-stop order must be placed ½ to 1½ points above the resistance points which make up the top of the line, and his sell-stop orders must be placed ½ to 1½ points below the support points which make up the bottom of the line.

Likewise, the necessity for the use of individual charts is evident in the proper determination and location of trend lines. When the movement of a stock breaks a well-defined advancing trend line, it is usually the sign of a reversal in trend. Upon breaking the bottom trend line of an advancing trend, the stock will shortly meet support and from that support point, a weak recovery movement ordinarily will take place with the volume of transactions drying up on this advance. When the short seller notices this advance faltering, he can sell short one-half of the number of shares he has anticipated selling short in that stock. This short sale should immediately be protected by a buy-stop order placed ½ to 1½ points above the top limit of this weak recovery movement.

The short seller should now place a sell-stop order about ½ point under the support point marking the breaking of the bottom trend line. When this support point is subsequently broken on the downside, his sell-stop order is touched off and he becomes short the second half of his desired short commitment. This type of operation will show the short seller a slight profit on the first half of his short sale before he becomes short of the full amount. This method of operation is very logical because the breaking of a bottom trend line is the sign that the upflow of the tide of stock price action is weakening and that, following a last weak upsurge, the subsequent breaking of the support level outside the bottom trend line definitely indicates that the ebb or downflow of price movement has begun.

As the price of the stock fluctuates in its downward wave surges, the short seller will be able to establish the major downtrend lines. These will be plotted on the extremities of the low points of the down surges, and on the extremities of the upsurges or recovery movements.

The short seller may add to his short commitments by shorting additional shares on the first two recovery movements, at a time when he sees such recovery movements exhaust themselves. He must, at all times, adequately protect his short position with a buy-stop order, lowering this buy-stop progressively, to above the recovery points as the stock declines.

When the stock breaks out of the downtrend line on the upside, it will either form a line or make a bottom formation. At this point, the short seller may decide to wait for the last weak down movement which usually moves into new low ground, accompanied by much less volume than accompanied the two previous downsurges. Such price action calls for immediate short covering. If the short seller does not cover his shorts during this price action of the stock, he must, at this point, be sure that his buy-stop orders above the market are closely placed, in order to protect the major portion of his short profits.

If the short seller wishes at this time to become a bull and profit by the impending advance, he will write "Buy____ Shares, Double Stop," on his order, instead of "Buy____ Shares, Stop." The latter type order will only cover his short position. The former type order, using the term Double Stop, will cover the short sale and buy a like amount of long stock when the buy-stop price is reached.

CONDITIONS SIGNALLING END OF A BULL MARKET*

Listed below are 36 conditions to be observed in determining whether fundamental, technical and psychological conditions are such that the top of a business cycle and the top of a bull market are approaching or being made. These observa-

*Editor's note: See Appendix A.

tions can not be made all at once, but must be made as they occur, which may require a period of six months to a year. A few of the observations will require a somewhat longer time. The recognition of these conditions, at or near the end of a four and one-half year cyclical upswing, raises warning signals that all is not well in the market place.

These conditions listed, represent economic fundamentals, technical conditions of the market itself and not the least important, the psychological attitudes of the investing and trading public. They are the conditions which forewarn of an approaching change of trend and a bear market.

One's decision to liquidate long stocks can not be made on just a few of the observations, but can be made when approximately twenty-five of the thirty-six conditions are observed to be in full force. During the observation of these conditions, paper profits should be protected by relatively close sell-stop orders which should be moved up as security prices spear higher and as bullish excesses occur.

The bull, instead of becoming more greedy, should be a little frightened at the rapid increase of his paper profits at this time. He should not reinstate a stock when "stopped out," nor buy other issues that are overpriced. The purchase of laggards or stocks which are behind the market is execeedingly dangerous at this time. He should nurture a cash position as he is progressively stopped out of his stocks, and hold that cash position in preparation for the bear campaign which he may contemplate.

It is during this period of six to eight months while a bull market top is being formed, that a bear campaign should be formulated. The choice of stock as candidates for short sales is treated elsewhere in this text.

Sell Signals During the End of the Bull Cycle—
Prosperity Top

1. Tremendous industrial production. Six to ten months' delivery on orders.

2. Great demand for labor. Labor shortages, even at extremely high wages.

3. Overexpansion of credit. New stock issues are no longer over-subscribed.

4. Many new offerings of securities by underwriters.

5. Over-evaluation of common stocks—many stocks selling to yield 2%, 2½%, 3%.

6. Persistent and rapid increase in commodity prices.

7. Many strikes for higher wages by relatively inefficient labor.

8. Both industry and labor have developed luxurious tastes.

9. Bond yields high. Bond prices low. But no one wants bonds because of inflated cost of living.

10. Real estate booms. The public is buying and selling real estate for profit.

11. Real estate is tremendously inflated. Exorbitant rents. Housing shortages.

12. A decrease in foreign trade. Attempts to bolster our exports by gifts.

13. Trade concessions to maintain full production for expanded capacities.

14. Business morality is low. Black markets. Sellers' market. Price gouging.

15. Tremendous construction awards, both industrial and private.

16. Inventories excessively high and maintained by large bank loans.

17. General confidence of the future which causes excessive productive capacity.

18. Enormous consumptive demand for all types of consumer goods.

19. Heavy industries are booming with no foreseeable let-up in demand.

20. Heavy exportation of gold. True only in free gold market.

21. Excessive bullish activity in gold mining shares. (Hedge against deflation.)

22. Increase in loan rate on call and time loans.

23. Increase in rediscount rates by Federal Reserve Board.

24. Increased margin demanded by brokers or Federal Reserve Board.

25. Corporate earnings very high. Extra dividends. Stock split-ups. Mergers.

26. Public participation in stock market is tremendous. Board rooms are full.

27. The stock market makes the "Front Page" for several weeks or months.

28. Abnormal increase in brokers' loans.

29. Irregularity (churning) of stock prices on extremely high volume.

30. Heavy volume on individual stocks with no appreciable gain in price.

31. Excessive bullish reports by industrial leaders.

32. Extravagant claims and tips on what certain stocks or averages will do.

33. Hundreds of new highs in forenoon and declines in afternoon on big volume.

34. Rapid run-ups (3 to 10 points per day) on high volume prior to the top.

35. Increased volume on declines with drying up of volume on price advances.

36. Distribution formations with "gaps" and volatile short covering movements.

CONDITIONS SIGNALLING END OF A BEAR MARKET

Thirty-six conditions which signal the end of a bear market and the end of a business depression are listed below. The bear, if he has not already covered or bought in his shorts, must do so when the majority of the listed conditions have been and are currently evident. These economic conditions, so evident, cannot long exist, particularly when they have reached their worst state.

A period of six to eight months, during the extreme bottom, is all the time that is given for the bear to cover his shorts and for him to make his choice of stocks which he will carry long during the approaching bull market. The choice of the stocks, as candidates for the impending bull campaign, is treated elsewhere in this text.

Buy Signals During The End of The Bear Cycle— Depression Bottom

1. Industrial production is at a low ebb. Immediate deliveries, at low prices.

2. Unemployment figures high. Factories working part time.

3. Credit is still tight. Difficult to raise capital by stock flotation.

4. Business failures reach new high. Building & Loans and Banks tighten credit.

5. Common stocks, selling at new lows, yield 5% to 8%. Dividends being omitted.

6. Commodity prices low. Prices of some will not pay the freight to market.

44

7. Very few strikes. Labor union membership low. Labor competes for jobs.

8. Labor and Industry have developed conservative and frugal habits.

9. Bond prices are low, with yields high. Many speculative bonds default.

10. Real estate prices low. Mortgages foreclosed. Difficult to sell real estate.

11. Rents have been reduced. Families have doubled up. Collections are bad.

12. Many stores and shops are vacant as a result of small business failures.

13. Everyone buying Government Bonds and Postal Savings, at low yield, for safety.

14. Busines morality high. Buyers' market. People pay cash or do without.

15. Construction awards low. Banks afraid to loan. General pessimism.

16. Inventories low. Competition aggressive. Margin of profit small, if any.

17. State and City governments running in the red. Tax collections poor.

18. Heavy industries have few orders. Eventual recovery seems impossible.

19. Debt moratoriums. Foreign trade practically nil.

20. Farm mortgages foreclosed. Farmers strike against foreclosures.

21. Senate makes investigations on "Bear raids" on commodity markets.

22. Government aid to Railroads and Industries to pay fixed charges. R.F.C. Loans.

23. Much money is hoarded. Fear of banks. Attempts to get people to spend.

24. Brokers' loans low. General fear of putting money into equities.

25. Stocks selling below quick assets.

26. Pessimistic reports and predictions. Public psychology is at a low ebb.

27. Rumors that Stock Exchange may close, that strong institutions totter.

28. Fear and hysteria cause runs on Building & Loans.

29. Minority groups march on Washington.

30. Volume of stock sales exceedingly low, 350,000-400,000 shares per day.

31. New lows for the averages bring out less stock on each successive downwave.

32. Certain leading stocks may show strong rallying tendencies.

33. Brokerage offices empty. Brokers close outlying branch offices.

34. Everyone thinks that the market will go lower. Many traders are short.

35. Volume increases as stocks rally and decreases as they sag back.

36. If buying equities seems the most hazardous and foolish thing you could possibly do, then you are near the bottom that will be the end of the bear market.

DOW-JONES AVERAGES

30 INDUSTRIALS

Allied Chemical
Alcoa
American Can
American Tel & Tel
American Tobacco
Anaconda
Bethlehem Steel
Chrysler
Du Pont
Eastman Kodak
General Electric
General Foods
General Motors
Goodyear
Inter Harvester

Inter Nickel
Inter Paper
Johns-Manville
Owens-Ill Glass
Procter & Gamble
Sears Roebuck
Std Oil of Calif
Std Oil of N J
Swift
Texaco
Union Carbide
United Aircraft
US Steel
Westinghouse El
Woolworth

20 RAILROADS

Atchison, Topeka
Atlantic Coast L
Baltimore & Ohio
Canadian Pacific
Ches & Ohio
Chicago & NW
Chi, Rk Is & Pac
Del & Hudson
Erie-Lackawanna
Great Northern

Illinois Central
Kansas City Sou
Louisville & N
NY Central
NY, C & St L
Norfolk & West
Pennsylvania
Southern Pacific
Southern Railway
Union Pacific

15 UTILITIES

Amer Elec Power
Cleveland E Ill
Colum Gas Sys
Comwlth Edison
Consol Edison
Consol Nat Gas
Detroit Edison

Houston Lt & Pow
Niag Mohawk P
Pacific Gas & El
Panhandle EPL
Peoples Gas
Phila Elec
Pub Serv E&G

Sou Cal Edison

The Dow-Jones Averages date back to 1896, and consisted of 20 Industrial stocks and 20 Railroad stocks during the "Roaring Twenties" and through 1929. A Utility Average consisting of 15 representative Utility stocks was added during the early Thirties. About the same time the D-J Industrial Average was increased to 30 stocks. The obvious divisor for this average was 30, but as subsequent stock split-ups occurred, the divisor was reduced after each split-up in order that the average would reflect the true course in relation to past fluctuations.

Stock split-ups, including Eastman Kodak, Johns-Manville, Chrysler, General Motors and U.S. Steel in recent years, have reduced the original divisor to below 10. With each subsequent split-up, the divisor will again be reduced. For this reason the daily fluctuations of the average will become greater as each additional split-up occurs.*

THE DOW THEORY

A knowledge of the Dow Theory is a great aid in investment and speculation. It is as important to the short seller as the long buyer. One reason why the author considers this theory valuable is because it has millions of almost fanatic adherents who, when acting in unison, cause periods of temporary market excesses in speculation which can be used by the more astute trader and investor to his advantage.

The Dow Theory is based on the observations of Mr. Charles Dow, made around the turn of the century. These observations show that an average of representative rail stocks seems to move with and confirm the action of an average of representative industrial stocks in establishing wave movements or trends.

The simplest way to explain the theory is to compare the movement of the Rail Average and the Industrial Average with the waves on the seashore which make up the ebb and flow of the tides. Each wave of the rising tide moves a little higher on the beach than the previous one. As each wave retreats, it recedes less than the last one. This wave pattern of succeeding higher points, both for the extent that the waves advance and the succeeding higher points that mark the end

* Editor's note: As of this writing, the following divisors are in use: Industrials, 2.914; Rails, 5.04; Utilities, 5.43.

of receding points, continues until the tide exhausts itself. This wave movement is comparable to the movement of the Averages in a bull market.

Contrarywise, the Dow Theory bear market can be compared to the ebb of the tide, during which each wave recedes lower than the last, and during which each advancing wave fails to advance on the beach as high as the previous one. This receding pattern continues until the ebb is finished and a change of tide or trend is observed.

Dow Theory confirmation of a change in trend from a bear market to a bull market comes at such a time when the wave movement of the Industrial Average, with the Rail Average confirming the action, refuses to recede lower than the last low point and, upon subsequent upswing, the movement is higher than the last high point. This is an indication that the ebb is completed and that a reversal of trend is in progress.

Dow Theory confirmation of a change in the trend from a bull market to a bear market occurs when, with both Averages confirming, the Averages fail to better their previous highs, and upon subsequent recession go lower than their last recovery point.

Every investor and speculator should have ready access to a chart of the movement of the Dow-Jones Averages which he can observe from time to time to keep himself posted on the market's action and on possible changes in trend. The author's preference for the Dow-Jones Averages is based upon his application of certain principles of the Dow Theory, as outlined in *The Dow Theory* by Mr. Robert Rhea. It is advisable that a thorough study of this theory be made in order to enhance one's knowledge of market movements.

When the Dow-Jones Rail and Industrial Averages move in such a manner as to give a Dow Theory confirmation of a bull or bear market trend and, more particularly, a signal of continuation of the trend then in force, then millions of Dow Theory followers will rush in emotionally and blindly to follow what they erroneously consider to be a Dow Theory buy or sell signal. Usually, to their chagrin, they find that they "followed the crowd" and made commitments at a time when the market has temporarily exhausted its technical strength by forcing itself up or down twenty or thirty points in order to break through the confirmation levels. There are many excellent opportunities for buying and short selling following the movement of the Averages to and through confirmation point levels, particularly when such a movement has been rapid and of such extent as to impair the technical strength of the movement.

The Dow Theory, as observed by Mr. Charles Dow and interpreted by Hamilton and Rhea, does not call out definite buy or sell signals. It does interpret the movement of the Averages as constituting changes of trends or confirmations of continuations of movement in those trends, but at no place does the theory say, "Buy immediately" or "Sell immediately," upon certain confirmation action of the Averages. The Theory merely suggests or theorizes that a certain trend action is likely to follow because of similar historical patterns so often repeated. In the author's opinion, those millions of Dow Theory adherents, who rush in madly to make commitments immediately when a Dow Theory signal is given, are making an interpretation which both Dow and Hamilton would consider improper. The very fact that the Theory has millions of adherents no doubt makes the Theory more fallacious as the number of its adherents increases from year to year.

The purpose here is not to expound on the Dow Theory or its controversial value. It is felt, however, that the Theory is of sufficient value that all investors and traders should be familiar with its tenets. Warning, however, is given here not to read into the Theory that which is not there, and to be wary of those advisory services which build up lists of buy or sell recommendations to be executed immediately upon the flash of a confirmation signal of the trend then in force.

A more logical and more profitable analysis is one which must be used as a supplement to the interpretation of the position of the Averages. This analysis is one in which you, as an anvestor or trader, will attempt to determine and measure the fundamental value of a stock, its technical position and the technical (overbought or oversold) position of the market averages. You will carefully scrutinize the current and future economic factors, and the current and probable psychological reactions of future buyers and sellers. This should be done to enable you to arrive at a more logical reason for buying stocks and timing their purchases, than is possible in blindly following the signals as registered by the movement of the Dow Averages.

A proper measure of these factors and a knowledge that you, as an investor or trader, must be an accommodating and obliging individual who is more than willing to sell and to satisfy the public's emotional, avid and seemingly insatiable appetite for stocks, at a time when yields are low and prices skyrocketing, will allow you to calmly retire from a long position on the basis of logical reasoning. From this neutral position you can assay the true proportions and weight of the remaining market strength or the inherent weakness of the technical and fundamental factors, with a calmness that comes only from a side line position. It is from this neutral position that it is possible for you to study the possibilities and evidence of a change in trend and, thereafter, to choose short sale candidates for the inevitable reaction or bear market that is to follow.

It is with the same side line poise that you, as an investor, in cash position, can subsequently observe that stocks are being frantically liquidated at high yields in a collapsing market. Such selling is so urgent (late tape) that you again calmly reason that you must obligingly accommodate these emotional sellers by buying some of the bargains which they are now dumping on the market.

The short seller, having much earlier satisfied those on an emotional buying spree by selling them short stock, now observes the emotional selling climax which prompts him also to quickly become an accommodating buyer. Thus he covers his short position and possibly becomes a buyer of long stock.

More often than not, such analysis, psychological approach, mental poise and the will to so oblige and to so accommodate will result in remarkable profits, far more in fact, than is possible from blindly following the Dow Theory, which requires exhaustive mass action and psychological excesses to accomplish the moves which make up the signals of confirmations.

TAPE READING

The tape records prices at which sellers and buyers agree to exchange stock for money and money for stock. Other records, such as those printed in the daily financial section of newspapers, charts and other financial sales data, are available to those who wish to draw their conclusions from such media, rather than by "sitting on the tape" daily at the broker's office.

A knowledge of tape reading is extremely desirable and profitable when properly used. Proper use is definitely not in sitting in a board room for five hours each day. In fact, the "tape worm" can not ordinarily subject himself to the tape recordings of the daily fluctuations without losing his perspective of the intermediate and major market movements.

The tape is of great aid and value when it is used to check and to verify conclusions arrived at by the use of charts and other data. Occasional hours spent observing the tape will clarify the importance of major news events and their effect on the market, and will make possible a wider experience in the correct evaluation of major news events.

The tape is a receptacle and clearing house for thousands of news items, tips, fears, greeds, rumors and conjectures. It records the immediate buying or selling action of those who are in a position to know of the first change, good or bad, in a company's fortunes. Almost every thing that is known or anticipated is recorded on the tape in terms of buying or selling orders many hours, days or even months before the newspapers, market letters and radio commentators can dispense the information to the public at large.

News leaks from the Nation's Capital are even preceded by tape recordings of purchases or sales by those who are in a position to know news before it becomes news. It is, therefore, essential that the trader realize the tape's action is the first and most important source of unknown information. The unknown information will be printed later in the newspapers, but the tape is recording that the unknown information is going to be either good or bad when printed. If the tape's action is strong, the news will generally be good, and if the tape's action is weak, the news will generally be bad.

It is a consistent and common observation by those who follow the market that rather strong upward movements and strong tape action usually culminates when the good news is out. Likewise, when the tape has recorded consistent selling pressure and sustained declining prices, such a move generally stops when the bad news, such as a reduction or omission of a dividend, is out. "When the news is out, it is unimportant." This old Wall Street axiom is based on a long period of observations that the tape and the market generally discount the news before it is published, and wise short sellers may utilize this phenomenon to enter and close short commitments.

Each purchase of stock—whether an odd-lot of 50 shares, matched with other odd-lots to complete a full trading unit of 100 shares, or orders consisting of 500, 1000 or 5000 shares —have their influence on the change of price of a particular stock. These buy orders affect the price change only in relation to the supply of stock at that particular time. The tape reader or chartist can ascertain whether it takes a demand for 1000 shares to put a stock up one point or whether it takes a demand for 15,000 shares to put the stock up a point. This is extremely important because it gives the trader a demand and supply action and relationship which he can analyze as moderate strength in the first instance, or as running into a supply or offering of stock in the second instance. In the latter instance, the trader knows that if the offerings persist at that level without demand increasing and overcoming the offerings, then the stock will decline from that level. A seasoned tape reader can discern this from tape action.

Every selling order, whether large or small, has its effect of stopping an advance or contributing to a decline. The effect is dependent upon the size of the selling orders in relation to the then-existing buy orders. If the offerings encounter what is known as a thin market—that is, very little demand within a certain radius—the price will decline in proportion to the overweight of the offerings. If the offerings are large and urgent and the market thin, a large gap opening may appear, and if the weight of the offerings persist, a substantial declining movement will result, which will be stopped only by a greater demand appearing at a lower level. When this level is reached, the tape reader or daily chartist will observe a great demand for thousands of shares of stock which overpowers the heavy liquidation. This is a signal for the bear to cover and for an immediate bullish operation. The market action at this particular time will usually show the price of the stock breaking into new low ground for the movement, and that the closing price of the stock will be a point or two points above the low of the day, and near or above the previous day's close. The volume of sales on this day must be extraordinarily heavy to make this an almost certain and valid turning point.

A stock is as strong as its closing price when its volume of transactions is increasing. In order for a stock to be considered strong by the tape reader or chartist, it must hold at least 50 per cent of its gain on a moderate increase in volume. If it holds more than 50 per cent of its gain, it shows added strength. This is particularly true after the stock has been depressed for some time. When a rapidly declining stock does not hold its loss, it shows that the underlying demand at that level is great, and a resilient bounce up from that level is evident and indicative that the stock is no longer weak. This action serves as a signal for shorts to cover.

Near the end of a bull market and after the rapid mark-up of prices in one stock after another, the resilient bounce-back of price can be noticed in many individual stocks and in the Averages. Under such conditions the public will have an avid appetite for stocks. During the heavy volume days at the top, the stocks and the Averages will go up into new high ground in the morning and will decline to near the previous day's close in the afternoon. Chart-wise, this action shows upward spear days with practically no gain on the day. This indicates that while the demand is heavy and urgent, the supply of stock is equally as great and the selling almost as urgent as the buying. It is from such volatile and resilient action at the top that the tape reader and chartist draws his conclusions that the turning point has arrived. It is after such action that the short seller is encouraged to start small ventures on the short side.

The main purpose of tape reading is to arrive at correct conclusions regarding the demand and the supply of stock at a particular time. For example, one can ascertain when the demand and supply are in perfect balance, for it is at such times that the market stops going up or stops going down. When accompanied by other factors, including heavy volume trading, this balance or equality of the selling pressure and the buying pressure marks turning points in the market at which time the investor or trader must act. During a period of such heavy transactions, if the market has had a sustained advance, his action will be that of selling, and if the market has had a rapid and devastating decline, his action will be that of buying.

To further explain the art of tape reading in detail, it is helpful to explore the manner in which a renowned professional speculator of a bygone era, whom we shall call Mr. Wondermore, made market tests in order to determine lines of least resistance. Mr. Wondermore spent most of his life, beginning as a youth in bucket shops, learning the laws of supply and demand and their effect on stock prices. Perhaps there has lived no figure in Wall Street history who knew better how to read the tape than Mr. Wondermore. It must be remembered that the market tests, explained below and made by him, were made to actually convince himself that he should be bullish on a stock or the market. Naturally, the size of his test commitments show that margins were extremely low at that time.

In the following market test it can be observed that Mr. Wondermore was trying to evaluate the forces of supply and demand. His and other traders' quotations appeared on the tape, so that a study of them gives a small beginning in the art of tape reading. Mr. Wondermore's mild bullishness at the beginning of his tests lacked positive conviction. Not until he tested the supply of stock above the market would he be certain of his bullish position.

J. C. Wondermore's Market Test

1. U.S. Steel is selling at $110 per share.
2. Mr. Wondermore placed an order to buy 2000 shares of Steel at the market.
3. If, as a result of his market order and those of a few other traders who are attracted by the tape recording of his purchase, the price advanced to 111, he immediately placed another buy order for another 2000 shares at the market.
4. If, as a result of his second 2000 share buy order, and those of others attracted by the advance and activity, Steel continued to go up to 112, he immediately placed a third order to buy 2000 shares at the market. He did this because so far he had been right. Most of his third 2000 share buy order was filled at 112¼.
5. From the impetus of the demand so created by the advance, Steel goes up steadily to 114. Mr. Wondermore now waits for a reaction which he expects to come back to the approximate price of his third purchase, which was at 112¼.
6. He now waits for a rally, beginning at approximately 112¼, which will advance the price to 113¾, just ¼ below its previous top of 114.
7. When the price reaches 113¾, he puts in a buy order, at the market, for 4000 shares.
8. If he gets his 4000 shares of Steel for 113¾, SOMETHING IS WRONG! He is running into a supply of stock. He now sells a 1000 share test order, at the market, to

see how well it is taken. If it is not well-taken, he may decide to retreat from his long position.

9. If, however, his 4000 share buy order at the market, placed when Steel was selling at 113¾, is filled in the following manner, he is absolutely SURE he is right:

2000 Shares at 114
  500   "   " 114½
  500   "   " 114¾
  400   "   " 115
  600   "   " 115½

You can readily see that Mr. Wondermore was not pleased when his orders were filled too cheaply and too easily, but was more certain of his bullish position if the stock which he bought was difficult to buy, except at advancing prices. This was proof that no great supply of stock was overhanging the market.

Mr. Wondermore, when bearishly inclined, would likewise test the underlying demand for stock by placing his short selling orders at the market, to see if such orders could depress the price easily or if his test orders were immediately absorbed by a great underlying demand. If they were absorbed without depressing the price, he would know that the line of least resistance was not on the downside but on the upside, and he would quickly cover his shorts and possibly go long of stock. If, however, his test orders proved that there was insufficient demand to absorb his short offerings, he would continue to offer more stock until he had completed the short line which he wished to carry. It must be pointed out that Mr. Wondermore lived during a time when there were no regulations on short selling, and thus short sales could be made as prices were declining.

It is obvious that market tests, such as those made by Mr. Wondermore, are being made each day, each week and each month, not by one particular skilled trader, but by the mass of buy and sell orders which come to the market from all sources. These tests are evident in individual stocks during all phases of their rhythm movements, whether in up or down trends during the formation of a line. When in a line, the tests to determine the greater force go on for some time. Some lines are completed in a few weeks and some may take six to nine months. The general rule applies that the greater the length of time in the line, the greater the move once the limits of the line are broken. The prudent investor or trader will sit on the side lines, watching the tape and his daily or weekly charts while these market tests are being made within the line. The more agile trader may attempt to buy on the support points and sell on the resistance points of the line, but he must realize that once the limits of the line are broken, he must immediately reverse his tactics.

Ordinarily, the fourth or fifth test of either the top level or the bottom level of a long line will be the test that is significant, since the fourth or fifth test will prove to be the one having sufficient force to break the limits of the line. This breakthrough will prove that there is either insufficient offerings at and above the upper limit of the line to stop an advance, or will prove that there is insufficient demand at and below the lower limit of the line to forestall a decline. The breakthrough of the limits of a line in either direction is the signal for the bull or the bear to act immediately, because it is at this time that the tape is giving him valuable information.

The average investor or trader does not have sufficient funds to conduct market tests of his own, so he must keenly observe and rely on those being made by others. In making these observations and in properly evaluating these tests, the investor or trader is, in a manner, imitating the tactics of Mr. Wondermore, in that he does not become certain of his bullish or bearish inclination until the line is broken, and

59

the demand and supply relationship is established by such a breakthrough and by such tape action.

There is a similarity in observing the forces at play as they are recorded on the tape, and in watching a good quarterback on a football team who is feeling out the opposing team for weak spots. The quarterback, after trying a dozen plays, knows whether he can most easily gain off tackle, around the end, through the air or through the center. He has found, by using test plays, certain weaknesses in opposing players which make possible his utilization of those weaknesses as a line of least resistance. He finds other men among the opposing players whom he cannot budge. The similarity of these tests on the gridiron are obvious to the tape reader who watches the constant battle of supply and demand as it is recorded on the tape. He notices, at one time, U.S. Steel with a tremendous force of demand, being stopped dead in its tracks by an equal amount of offerings. He may notice, at another time, that a play is directed at Chrysler and that the supply, as the price rises, is insufficient to withstand the force of an increasing demand, and a good gain is marked up. At still another time, a play is directed at General Motors, only to be quickly smothered by an avalanche of offerings which throw the price for a substantial loss.

The student of tape reading will do well to remember the above comparison, because it will aid him in translating the seemingly incomprehensible recordings of numbers and symbols. As he attempts to learn the art of tape reading, he can readily see that the market is constantly being tested.

Individual stocks are constantly being tested for weakness, strength or for public response. It makes no difference from whence the demand or supply comes. It may come from a frightened public or it may come from an investment trust. Always, however, it is recorded on the tape, and tells its story to those who become clever enough to understand it.

It is suggested that those wishing to make a detailed study of tape reading will find valuable aid in Mr. Humphrey B. Neill's book entitled, *Tape Reading and Market Tactics.*

THE BUYERS' STRIKE

A buyers' strike is a phenomenon which occurs during the last stages of an inflation cycle when the cost of living index, rising faster than wages, accentuates the spread between the two to such an extent, that people must augment their wages by dipping into savings in order to attempt to maintain their standard of living. People will thus tend to spend from savings up to a certain point at which they realize they are rapidly depleting their resources, and then, suddenly, almost acting in unison, they revise their buying habits and refuse to continue to dip into their savings, and begin postponing all but their absolutely necessary purchases.

The buyers' strike is accentuated by the first reduction in weekly working hours. A man on a six-day working week is suddenly cut back to a five-day week, thus losing the Saturday's time and one-half wages to which he has been accustimed and which has governed his spending habits. This immediately makes necessary a revision in his buying habits.

An additional influence, which is historically a powerful one, is the habit of people to postpone purchases upon the first signs of price reductions, in the hope that if they wait, prices will go lower and yet still lower. Not until they are convinced that prices have stopped going down will they begin spending in a normal way.

The knowledge that a buyers' strike is beginning is of first importance to anyone interested in the security or commodity markets, because it means a rapid decline in almost all prices as merchants, wholesalers and manufacturers try quickly, by price cutting, to reduce high cost inventories at

61

the highest possible price they can get and before lower prices prevail.

The buyers' strike is of such importance that if it applies to 30 per cent of purchasers, it will bring about a complete collapse in business and will drastically deflate commodity and security markets. For this reason, it is imperative that both the bull and bear take cognizance of the first signs of buyer resistance and price cutting. Perhaps the first and best indication of buyer resistance will come from mail order catalogs and newspaper advertisements of the large department stores which will show attempts to move large inventories at price reductions. A good indication is when competing stores try to push their sale dates ahead of their competitors' sale, by advertising price slashes in pre-Thanksgiving, pre-Christmas, pre-holiday sales of a nature that spells out worry over heavy and costly inventories. This is an indication that the consumer's dollar is getting scarce and that everyone is trying to get it first. Within six to eight weeks after such indications, a downturn in business can be expected, accompanied by greater accentuation of inventory liquidation sales and price cutting.

The bull will do well to be on the side lines during such a buyers' strike, and the bear will indeed be fortunate if he gets his short position just before the buyers' strike begins, because there will also follow a tendency toward a buyers' strike in stocks. There will be considerable liquidation of stocks caused by fear of top-heavy costly inventories being liquidated below cost, resulting in reduced profits or losses for the companies holding them. The threat of reduction of current dividends naturally follows from inventory losses and lower sales volume.

A similar buyers' strike—perhaps it should be called a postponement of building expansion plans by industries— takes place about the same period in the cycle. Nothing will halt building expansion plans quicker than the realization that inventories are not moving as they did formerly, and that plant production capacity may, after all, be sufficient for some time to come. A further realization that building and equipment costs may be lower one or two years hence will further curtail such expenditures.

Plant and equipment expansion has heretofore been based upon a demand that seemed impossible to satisfy. Plants and equipment were built with black or gray market steel at watered labor costs. Suddenly, evidence of a buyers' strike appears. Black market prices, grey market prices for steel, suddenly become actual mill prices. Cancellation of orders causes mill prices to be cut and the deflation cycle is well under way. Not until prices recede to a point where buying in a normal fashion reappears will the deflation cycle be completed.

THE BUSINESS CYCLE

Before any investor or speculator takes a position, either long or short, in the security markets he should be completely familiar with the five normal stages of a business cycle. To disregard an analysis of the current stage of the business cycle is to disregard the basic economic fundamentals which motivate the establishment of the bull and bear trends in security prices. Without proper knowledge of the major and intermediate trends in force, the investor-speculator is hopelessly lost. One cannot disregard economic trends, except for short term trading, without sooner or later being punished for such disregard.

In reviewing the forty items listed below, which constitute descriptions of particular economic conditions in the various stages of the business cycle, it will be observed that each item or condition has some direct economic influence on the condition which follows it. This relationship or influence always denotes certain changes which are taking place. These changes are the economic forces at play in a near (?) free economy, which are controlled by the economic and psychological effects of the application of the natural law of supply and demand and Sir Isaac Newton's law of action and reaction.

For a measure of the particular time, extent and position in which we might find ourselves in any one of the five stages of the business cycle, we must correlate the prevailing conditions with the observation of security and other price movements as represented by various charts which reflect that position. This is essential for proper determination of time and extent relationships in the business cycles.

The author believes there is no better index of the business cycle than the movements of a recognized stock market average. The most widely published of such averages are the Dow-Jones Industrial, Rail, Utility and Composite Averages. Since the prices of stocks listed on the New York Stock Exchange represent an expert appraisal of the stocks' actual and potential value, based on their individual and collective earning prospects for a particular phase of the business cycle, an average of such stocks, representing a cross section of American business enterprise, will attempt constantly to correctly evaluate the future earning potential of the stocks in such an average. It is for this reason that the term "discounting the future" is used to describe a vigorous trend in the Averages, which indicates that either business and trade will expand and flourish following a bullish market movement, or will decline and stagnate after a bearish impetus of sufficient magnitude has been portrayed in the movement of the Averages.

Every market movement has its particular meaning in relation to various stages of the business cycle. It is essential to remember that the Averages are always predicting, always evaluating, always re-evaluating, always discounting in advance the changing conditions in the state of our national and international financial and economic structures.

FIVE STAGES OF THE BUSINESS CYCLE

I. Boom and Credit Crisis

1. Good times and healthy conditions breed confidence and rising prices.
2. Confidence encourages borrowing from banks and breeds expansion.
3. Expansion leads to increased production, increased salaries and wages which are paid out before new production is completed.
4. Increased wages cause increased consumption.
5. Increased consumption causes additional orders to be placed.
6. Lowered stock of goods causes more borrowing and expansion.
7. General prosperity causes elation, extravagance, speculation, higher unit costs and higher operating ratios.
8. Enormous expansion causes an extraordinary output which now gluts the market, or which cannot be carried with available credit.

II. Collapse

9. Banks, skeptical of excessively high-priced inventories, refuse to make further loans to carry such inventories.
10. Refusal of credit causes cutbacks in production and layoffs.
11. Layoffs reduce purchasing power and demand.
12. Reduced demand causes further cutbacks and more layoffs.

13. Unit prices are reduced to move inventories, even at a loss.
14. People give up extravagant tastes and start to save, if possible.
15. Fewer orders are received by the manufacturers.

III. Depression

16. Inventories are gradually worked off at losses.
17. Middlemen's inventories get low.
18. Retailers' inventories get low.
19. Pessimism increases, all confidence disappears.
20. Bad trade leads to further price cutting.
21. Increased efficiency and reduction of unit cost is stressed.
22. Banks' position strengthens, because less money is used in trade.
23. Depression breeds efficiency among workers.
24. Consumers' goods wear out. Capital goods wear out.

IV. Revival

25. Eventually a point is reached where continued consumption, facilitated by gradual re-expansion of bank credit, eats into stocks of commodities faster than they are produced.
26. Retailers and wholesalers give more orders to produce.
27. Shipments of more goods require repair of freight cars.
28. Railroad repair depots call back crews, order more steel.
29. Steel mills recall workers and order more ore and coal.
30. Miners and steel workers buy new tools and necessities.
31. Freight shipments require new trucks, trailers and railroad cars.
32. More steel is ordered.

V. Prosperity

33. Employment increases and gradually confidence is restored.

34. Corporate earnings increase and workmen strike for more money.
35. Increased wages are granted because orders for goods are expanding.
36. Government projects now aid boost in employment and demand.
37. Unemployment is reduced and gradually disappears.
38. Additional strikes for higher wages; granted.
39. More building. More expansion. More credit. More production.
40. Everyone is employed. Scarcity of labor. Healthy, prosperous times are in evidence everywhere and the "Business Cycle" is complete.

DON'TS FOR THE BULL

1. Don't put a stock away and forget it.
2. Don't buy on thin margin.
3. Don't trade in stocks without limiting your risk with stops.
4. Don't always trade on the long side. Don't be a Perpetual Bull.
5. Don't sell a quiet market during a bull market.
6. Don't discuss your holdings with others.
7. Don't give opinions or tips.
8. Don't be afraid to quit the market.
9. Don't follow the crowd during market excesses.
10. Don't buy for income exclusively.
11. Don't buy "sympathy" stocks.
12. Don't buy stocks during resting periods.
13. Don't operate for the purpose of making trades.
14. Don't buy unless your chances are for a sizable move.
15. Don't buy unlisted stocks unless they are fire insurance stocks.

16. Don't put all your money in one company or one industry.
17. Don't answer a margin call. Sell some stock.
18. Don't hesitate to stay out of the market until you have firm convictions.
19. Don't buy or sell until the odds (based on yield) are in your favor.
20. Don't rely on information from an underwriting house on new issues.
21. Don't neglect to watch the action of Chrysler, General Motors and U.S. Steel.
22. Don't forget that convertible preferreds have a "sweetner" added.
23. Don't put yourself under obligation to the salesman of an underwriting house.
24. Don't buy new issues, as too many risks are involved.
25. Don't look upon investment funds as a possible source for meeting margin calls.
26. Don't be a bull in a bear market.
27. Don't be long and short at the same time, except as a hedge.
28. Don't get married to a stock.
29. Don't be a hog.

DON'TS FOR THE BEAR

1. Don't sell short without a stop-loss order.
2. Don't be a bear in a bull market.
3. Don't short small capitalization shares.
4. Don't over-extend yourself on the short side.
5. Don't short a strong "dog."
6. Don't short except in a cyclical downtrend.
7. Don't expect to cover at the exact bottom.
8. Don't take small short profits.

9. Don't expect to be right more than seven out of ten times.
10. Don't short unless you have a good reason to do so.
11. Don't sell too late; sell promptly or not at all.
12. Don't short "sympathy" stocks.
13. Don't short on strike news.
14. Don't short on "the" bad news.
15. Don't short the strong stocks. There are plenty of weak ones.
16. Don't let a short profit of over 20 per cent run into a loss.
17. Don't short when the technical condition is strong.
18. Don't short an issue having a large short interest, without reason.
19. Don't short stocks requiring a loaning premium.
20. Don't short unless your chart dictates selling.
21. Don't sell short too early or too late.
22. Don't expect an immediate crash after your short sale.
23. Don't switch to the bull side if your bear reasons are sound.
24. Don't expect your timing to be perfect.
25. Don't be dismayed if you must try several times to get a bear position.

CONCLUSION

There has been a definite attempt by the author to condense as much specific subject matter as possible in this book. In doing so, the opportunity of completely expanding each subject has been lost. Since the subject of money management, investment and speculation in its many and divers ramifications has become one of the broadest of the inexact sciences, this book can only serve to add light on several small facets of this broad subject.

The reader should realize that "a little knowledge is a dangerous thing," and should strive to further his study and experience from the many texts written on investment practices. Unfortunately, he will not find a great amount of material that has been written upon the subject of short selling, and it has been for that reason that the subject of short selling was chosen for presentation here.

It is hoped that the reader will have found herein some methods of analysis, some aspects of psychological approach and some prudent rationalizations on the technical and fundamental facets of investment and trading which will aid him in a more proper utilization and conservation of capital.

THE AUTHOR

APPENDIX

by The Editors of *Indicator Digest*

A

SELL SIGNALS AT BULL MARKET PEAKS

Most of the signals listed by Mark Weaver in this volume relate to the peak of a business cycle and are *fundamental* signs. They were well worth heeding when the work was written, and will be again whenever business booms reach the point of excess in future cycles.

There are, however, a number of *technical* stock market signals that may show up in advance of a major bear market, and often ahead of the economic signs. This is in keeping with the market's function of attempting to discount business slumps well in advance. Corporate "insiders" are usually the first to know when business has "topped out," long before it becomes apparent in the various business indices; these are past history by the time they appear on the financial pages. The resulting wholesale distribution of stock by these insiders is a frequent cause of some of the advance signals to be found in technical indicators.

Following is a list of technical signals apt to show up at bull market peaks, prepared by The Editors of *Indicator Digest*. Included are many of the signs that were present just prior to the 1962 decline.* Not all of these technical signals may appear; if more than half of them do, however, the exercise of extreme caution would be called for. Practically all of these figures can be gleaned from, or determined with, the figures published weekly in *Barron's*, or daily in *The Wall Street Journal* and in the financial sections of some leading newspapers, such as *The New York Times*. These and other significant technical signals are reported on and dis-

*Indicator Digest, an investment advisory service located in Palisades Park, New Jersey, was one of the few services to anticipate the mid-1962 market crash well in advance; it headlined a major sell signal in January 1962, when the Dow-Jones Average was still close to its peak.

cussed regularly in the pages of *Indicator Digest*.

Here, then, are technical sell signals that may be found at bull market peaks:

(1) The chart of the Dow-Jones Industrial Average shows it has finished the steep, almost vertical phase of its major advance, and now has established a sort of top "saw-tooth" pattern of large swings up and down, although still reaching for new bull market highs.

(2) The monthly Short Interest announced by the N. Y. Stock Exchange has gradually dropped 40 or 50 per cent of its bull market rise. The entire amount of shares in the Short Interest is far less than an average day's trading volume.

(3) In spite of the D. J. Average still making new highs, individual stocks show a total of daily New Highs far less than they showed earlier in the bull market, and on market dips we now are apt to see more New Lows than New Highs.

(4) Price/earnings ratios of many "glamour stocks" have gone to ridiculous heights—60, 80, 100 to 1 and more in some cases; the average Price/Earnings Ratio of the 30 stocks in the D. J. Industrial Average has climbed to a range between 20 and 25 to 1.

(5) Days when advances outnumber declines by 400 or more on the NYSE are now a rarity.

(6) The total amount of money in margin accounts, announced each month by the NYSE as "Net Debit Balances," has reached a peak and is now starting to drop. At the same time, "Free Credit Balances," showing the free cash held in customers' accounts by brokers, is dropping steeply each month, indicating that the public is using up its cash at a greater rate to buy stocks.

(7) Daily odd-lot figures show that the small odd-lot buyers are buying much more than they are selling, partic-

ularly during sharp market upsurges. The ratio of odd-lot transactions to total daily trading volume has risen sharply. Odd-lotters have become too timid to sell short, and the daily figures of odd-lot short sales have sunk to low levels, perhaps to less than 1000 shares.

(8) *Barron's* "Confidence Index" has been declining steadily for several months, indicating that "smart money" is now "playing it safe" by switching from speculative bond issues into gilt-edge bonds.

(9) The mass of stocks in general is not performing nearly as well as the Dow-Jones Industrial Average—brokers' customer's men keep hearing the same complaint: "I know the market is higher—but why are *my* stocks dropping?"

(10) Airline, Auto, Truck, Paperboard, Machine Tool, and Broadcasting stocks—the notorious "early top-outers"— have started resisting further advance.

(11) Low-priced stocks—the "cats and dogs"—had their field day some time ago, and topped out while the bull market was still raging; they now attempt to rally, but fail to make new highs.

(12) Average daily trading volume is far less than it was when the bull market was younger and more vigorous.

(13) The price of seats on the N. Y. Stock Exchange has dropped noticeably.

(14) The classic "Dow Theory" bear market signal, usually a late signal: The D. J. Industrial and Rail Averages (the signal must be rendered by *both* of them) have had a secondary downswing and risen again, but turn down before reaching their former highs; on the second downswing they fall to a point lower than on the previous secondary downswing, this being the actual Dow signal.

B

HOW TO SELECT THE BEST SHORT SALE
CANDIDATES

Short selling is a risky business, but those in a position to do a little homework can weed out the most logical candidates for profitable shorting during bear markets. To traders there is nothing more satisfying than having a good short position in a bear market, because stocks fall much faster than they rise, and in many cases a good short may be held for the long pull if it is obviously in a long major downtrending chart pattern. Novices are advised to stay away from shorting, or at least to experiment on paper first, until they feel thoroughly familiar with the technique.

Our Number One rule for short sellers is: Protect your short positions against more than a ten per cent loss with a stop-buy order placed with your broker *at the time you make the short sale.*

To select the best shorts, a chart book—one of the bar-chart services (such as *Trendline* or *Mansfield*)—is a must; your broker should have one if you do not. Go through the book and list those stocks that meet all of the following requirements:

(1) The stock must have had a large rise in recent months —preferably an emotional rise, not founded on fact or reality.

(2) The rise was on increased volume; thus, it can be anticipated that many people will rush to protect their paper profits when the stock starts breaking down (falling below the top area).

(3) The stock must have stopped rising at least three weeks ago, preferably longer.

(4) It must show a top area of distribution (large volume at the top, but unable to rise any higher), and must recently have started breaking down.

(5) The stock has not declined more than ten per cent from its secondary peak as yet.

(6) The stock must now have a Price/Earnings Ratio of at least 25:1 (this can be determined from earnings listed in *Barron's*).

(7) The number of shares of common stock listed for the stock should be at least three million, as stocks too thinly capitalized can run up too quickly in a rally.

(8) The stock should have a low short interest, preferably less than one-half of one per cent of its common stock capitalization (short interest is listed once a month, shortly after the 15th, in *Barron's* and *The Wall Street Journal*).

Once you have listed stocks meeting these criteria, then give preference to those that:

(9) Show greatest downside volatility in past chart action.

(10) Are in industries on the downgrade (see *Indicator Digest's* monthly Industry Group Surveys).

(11) Have just completed a very bearish chart pattern, such as a "double-top" or "head-and-shoulders."

(12) Are very popular, widely traded.

One final rule: Once you have a profit on paper, keep a *trailing* stop-buy order on your short at the point where it would decisively break out of its downward channel.

C

SHORT SELLING FROM CHARTS, USING VOLUME AS A GUIDE

As many traders have observed, a stock which experiences an enormous surge of trading volume at the end of a short, steep move usually has a sizable dip shortly thereafter, due to the technical condition of the stock. At the peak of its volume surge, the supply of stock in "weak hands" is enormous, as the large volume was produced by the attraction of short-term traders, and these traders are sure to take profits as soon as the stock resists further rise. By looking through a weekly stock chart service (such as *Trendline* or *Mansfield*), you can spot these unnatural volume budges instantly. These are especially apt to be profitable among speculative stocks of low quality, particularly those selling at between $8 and $20 per share on the American Stock Exchange.

This trading technique, which is well known among stock exchange floor traders, should be governed by the following rules:

(1) The prospective stock is a speculator's medium, rather than a blue chip. (2) It recently had a steep, wild upward spurt for three or four consecutive weeks, which now apparently is spent. (3) Its peak volume, shown by an unusually tall volume bar at the bottom of the stock chart, appeared in the last week of the short rise. The volume for that week is at least 400 per cent or 500 per cent of the stock's average trading volume shown by the other volume bars. (4) Following the peak week, the stock usually goes sideways for a week or two in a short consolidation phase as new buyers, attracted by the wild surge, are met head-on by those taking profits. *The precise moment to go short occurs at the end of this consolidation stage when the stock takes its first sizable daily dip.* But first make certain that (5) the number of shares of

common stock listed for the stock is 3 million or more, and that (6) its last monthly short interest figure (which is published in *Barron's* or *The Wall Street Journal*) is not more than ½ of 1 per cent of this common stock capitalization. (Rules 5 and 6 help safeguard against a sudden volatile "whipsaw" movement of the stock.) (7) Always place a stop-buy order with your broker at the same time you transact the short sale. This should be placed a point or two above the peak price level attained during the surge.

The best timing for such transactions is achieved by waiting for what is obviously the start of a general secondary market downswing, usually determined by the signals of the short-term indicators (reported regularly in *Indicator Digest*). Such stock can then be shorted even in bull markets. When the secondary market trend is uncertain, many traders hedge by shorting vulnerable stocks of this type while remaining long in contra-trend market leaders.

When to Cover Shorts

Following the short consolidation at the top, the stock will generally begin a gradual decline and then, after a while, have a short downward plunge of one or two weeks, as traders begin to realize the advance is over and rush to protect their profit. As a rule, this plunge will end on a selling climax of one or two days as the stock reaches a temporary low on larger volume. This shakeout will arrest the decline for the time being, as it exhausts the supply of stock. As confirmation of this exhaustion, the stock will resume going sideways or start rising. *The very start of this new phase, following the selling climax, is the precise time to cover.*

In selecting stocks of this type, always give preference to those showing negligble earnings and unusually high price/earnings ratios; many such stocks on the American Stock

Exchange will show current earnings deficits. Particularly avoid stocks that have risen for only one week, as the rise is likely to be resumed even though temporary profit-taking may have appeared.

Examination of the chart books will reveal the surprisingly large percentage of profitable trades that could have been made by this method. If nothing else, you will become aware of the vital trading principle known to many professionals but overlooked by the general public: *Sufficient volume will kill off any advance, whether in an individual stock or in the averages.* This knowledge can serve as an important guide not only in short selling but in helping to determine the best time to buy an advancing stock, as well.

D

"CREEPING" SHORTS

Most traders usually look for the highly volatile issues as short sale vehicles, attempting to cash in on the huge downward plunges such stocks often have. Many traders have learned to their sorrow that they can get "whipsawed" in these stocks which can turn around just as violently when the market rallies, resulting in staggering losses for short sellers.

Much larger profits have been realized on the short side by smart professionals who get into short positions for the *long pull* in a bear market, using as their media the type of stocks we call *creeping shorts*. These can be readily selected by a perusal of chart books, and are characterized by a long, slow, downward trend which retains its angle even during sharp secondary market rallies. *They are usually ignored by odd-lot short sellers*, because they are not volatile enough, and for many days their movements seem almost imperceptible. Yet the relentless erosion persists week after week, month after month. Such stocks are usually endowed with unusually small short interests, and all recent support levels on their charts have, in most cases, been violated so that there is nothing in sight to stop their downdrift. Also, on the theory that the price action of stocks reveals the sum total of everything that everyone knows about a company, we gather that all may not be well with the earnings picture of many of these companies.

E

THE "PANIC LEVEL" IN SHORT SELLING

Those who have access to daily or weekly charts of individual stocks can easily find the "Panic Level" at which the rate of decline of a stock is apt to accelerate quite sharply. This especially applies to the "runaway" type of stock that has had an unusually steep advance on heavy volume sometime in the past few months.

The Panic Level is found by determining the price range at which the heaviest volume came in. For example, let us say that stock XYZ rose from $20 to $40 per share, and that the heaviest volume (as shown on the bottom of the stock chart) came in from $25 all the way up to $35. As XYZ tops out, it is likely to back and fill indecisively from its peak of $40 down to $35, showing only a mild downtrend during this period. The moment it gets into the heavy volume range, however (i.e., below $35), traders who purchased between $25 and $35 will become worried and start dumping their stock to protect paper profits. It is at this point that the decline of a speculative stock picks up in intensity, and the stock begins losing one or more points daily instead of fractions. The greater the volume had been in the $25-$35 range, the more the selling pressure will be when the stock gets back into that range again. In conclusion, when the stock declines and comes close to its Panic Level range, it becomes a most intriguing short sale possibility because it is approaching the area of greatest downside volatility. It also follows that short-term traders should cover shorts somewhere in the middle of this range, at the precise point where the downside volume has assumed climactic proportions and the stock begins to steady after a series of steep daily drops.

81